DOUBLE**WEDDING RING**

LOGCABIN

OHIO**STAR**

Editor's Choice New Quilts from an Old Favorite

American Quilter's Society

P. O. Box 3290 • Paducah, KY 42002-3290

www.AQSquilt.com

Located in Paducah, Kentucky, the American Quilter's Society (AQS) is dedicated to promoting the accomplishments of today's quilters. Through its publications and events, AQS strives to honor today's quiltmakers and their work and to inspire future creativity and innovation in quiltmaking.

Editor: Barbara Smith
Graphic Design: Lisa M. Clark
Cover Design: Michael Buckingham
Photography: Charles R. Lynch

Library of Congress Cataloging-in-Publication Data

Editor's choice : new quilts from an old favorite contest : double wedding ring, log cabin, Ohio star / by the American Quilter's Society ; [Barbara Smith, editor].
    p. cm.
    ISBN 1-57432-804-2
    1. Patchwork--Patterns.   2. Quilting--Patterns.   3. Patchwork quilts--Competitions--United States.   4. Double wedding ring quilts.   5. Log cabin quilts.   6. Star quilts.   I. Smith, Barbara, 1941-   II. American Quilter's Society.
    TT835 .E37737 2002
    746.46'041--dc21

                                2002005001

Additional copies of this book may be ordered from the American Quilter's Society, PO Box 3290, Paducah, KY 42002-3290 or online at www.AQSquilt.com.

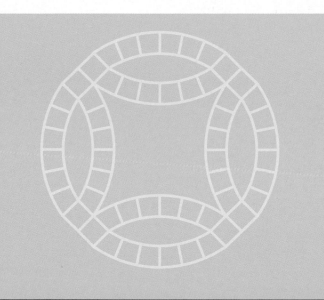

The Museum

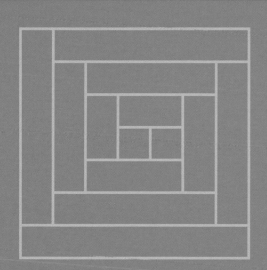

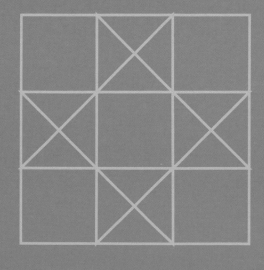

A dream long held by American Quilter's Society founders Bill and Meredith Schroeder and by quilters worldwide was realized on April 25, 1991, when the Museum of the American Quilter's Society (MAQS, pronounced "Max") opened its doors in Paducah, Kentucky. As stated in brass lettering over the building's entrance, this non-profit institution is dedicated to "honoring today's quilter" by stimulating and supporting the study, appreciation, and development of quiltmaking throughout the world.

The 30,000-square-foot facility includes a central exhibition gallery featuring a selection from the 135 quilts by contemporary quiltmakers comprising the museum's permanent collection, and two additional galleries displaying changing exhibits of antique and contemporary quilts. Lectures, workshops, and other related activities are also held on site in spacious modern classrooms. A gift and book shop makes available a wide selection of fine crafts and quilt books. The museum is open year-round and is handicapped accessible.

For more information, write MAQS, P.O. Box 1540, Paducah, KY 42002-1540 or phone 270-442-8856.

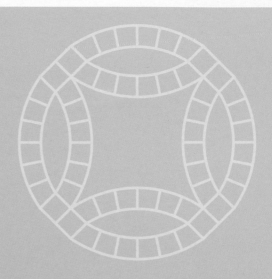
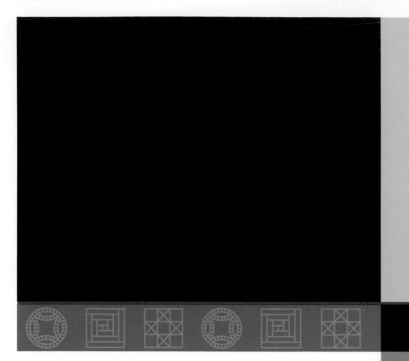

Contents

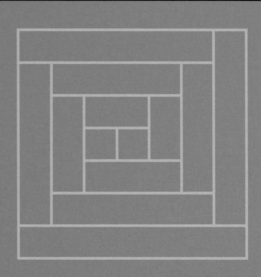

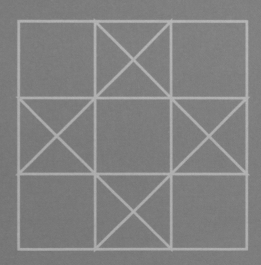

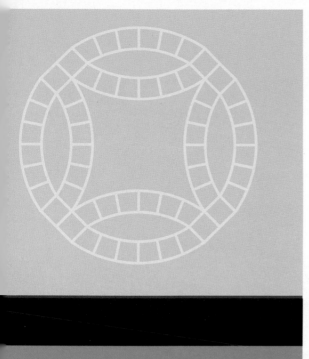

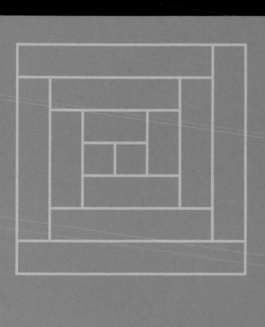

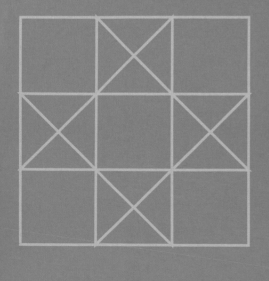

INTRODUCTION

Every year since 1993, the Museum of the American Quilter's Society has challenged quiltmakers to create innovative quilts based on a traditional block pattern. The winners and finalists of the New Quilts from an Old Favorite contest are first exhibited at the museum, and then the exhibit travels to a number of museums across North America, where it is viewed by thousands of quilt enthusiasts. Each year, AQS publishes a book featuring the 18 winners and finalists.

Editor's Choice is a compilation of six selections from each of the three most popular contest books, which are now out of print: *Double Wedding Ring Quilts* (1994), *Log Cabin Quilts* (1995), and *Ohio Star Quilts* (1996).

Although the contest encourages "outside the box" creativity, there were some basic requirements for entries:

• The quiltmakers needed to use the contest block in a way that it was still recognizable.

• The minimum finished quilt width and length was 50". The maximum was 100".

• Each quilt was required to be quilted.

• A quilt could be entered only by the person or persons who made it.

• Each quilt had to be completed within the time specified by the contest.

Full-color quilt photographs are accompanied by the quiltmakers' statements. Their comments provide insight into their widely divergent creative processes. Full-sized patterns for blocks of several sizes are also included to form the basis for your own interpretation.

DOUBLE WEDDING RING QUILTS

The Double Wedding Ring pattern, with its curved interlocking circles, offers shapes and spaces different from those found in most pieced patterns. Some quilters find the prospect of piecing its many curves and angles intimidating and tell of avoiding use of the pattern. Others find the very same components challenging.

In some cases, the quilts entered in this contest were projects that had already been underway at the time the contest was announced. In other cases, they had already been completed. The Double Wedding Ring pattern is one quiltmakers often turn to when they are making a quilt to commemorate a special person or occasion.

A number of quilts entered in the competition were inspired by the contest theme. Many quilters commented that they had always intended to make a quilt based on the Double Wedding Ring pattern but had never actually done it. This contest provided just the incentive they needed to make one. Still other quilts were the result of a combination of the desire to enter the contest and a desire to commemorate a special anniversary.

In at least one case, the pattern is one that the quiltmaker has been exploring for a period of time, and several winners have remarked that they have found the Double Wedding Ring pattern so interesting that they are in the midst of a new series of quilts, all based on that pattern.

Some of the quilters have retained much from the traditional design, modifying only slightly the pieced structure and usual use of the design. Other quilters have boldly moved in new directions, re-interpreting the design quite dramatically. The quilts are a wonderful reminder of the latitude that traditional patterns offer quiltmakers. These patterns are there to be followed to whatever degree the maker wishes. And regardless of the degree of modification, the results can be spectacular.

AN EVER-FIXED MARK

51" x 60", Silks, cottons, reflective synthetic
Machine pieced & hand quilted

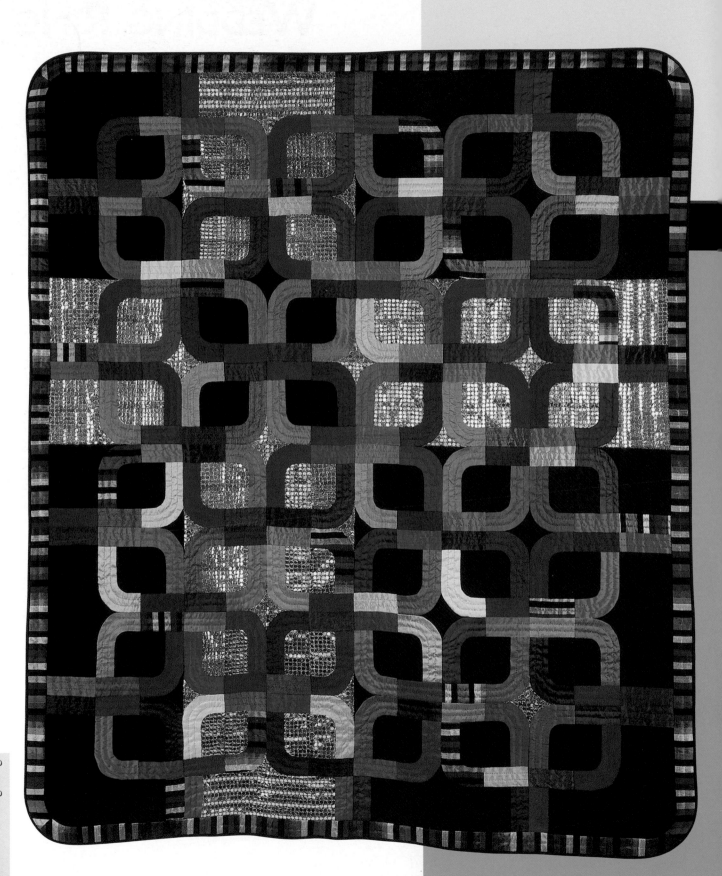

Marilyn Henrion

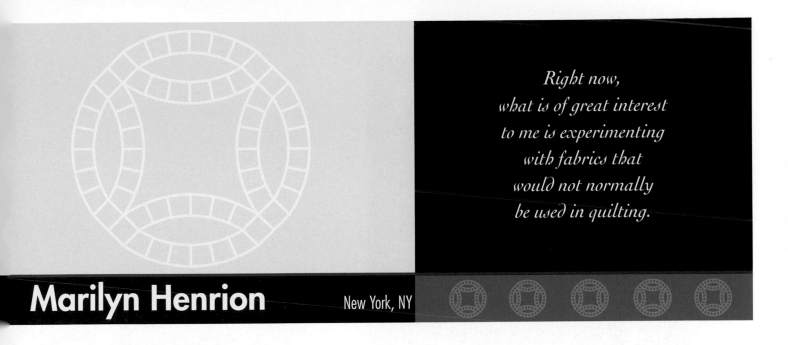

*Right now,
what is of great interest
to me is experimenting
with fabrics that
would not normally
be used in quilting.*

Marilyn Henrion
New York, NY

MY QUILTMAKING

Quilting brings together everything I love: fabric, color, mathematics, design, poetry, music. I find there is no end to my satisfaction with making quilts.

I started making them as legacies for my four children, to leave something of me when I'm gone. Self-taught, I learned from magazines like *American Quilter*. My background was in graphic design, so the design training was there, but the techniques I learned from publications. I had been quilting for 12 years before I took a workshop.

MY QUILT

When this MAQS competition was announced, I decided to develop an adaptation of the first orig inal design quilt I had made. Working with this Double Wedding Ring style design also seemed a nice way to celebrate the fact that, as of 1993, my husband and I had been married 41 years.

I liked working with the Double Wedding Ring design. It is complex enough to keep me interested. Machine piecing the curves takes a bit of practice, but once you've stitched a number of them, you become quite adept.

One of the more difficult things about making this quilt was the fabric. The silk I used tended to fray easily, so when I was piecing the curves and flipping them, there was fraying. I had to be a little more careful than with cotton.

I was surprised to discover that the reflective synthetic fabric in this quilt could be pieced. It's a knit fabric with circles glued on so strongly that they are an integral part of the fabric. Seeing the fabric on the bolt, I was so excited that I bought it not knowing if it would work in a quilt. The fabric required a little extra care, but I was able to stitch right through the little circles and could even hand quilt between them.

Working with that unusual fabric has made me want to experiment more with different types of fabric. At the moment, I am quilting a piece made of linen, and I find myself wondering why this fabric hasn't been used more in quilts. It is exciting to consider all of the other fabrics that could be used.

MY DESIGN

My original design involved a more elongated block like the one shown in the quilt drawing on page 10. Ultimately, I used the block shown at the top of page 10. The patterns on page 11 can be used to re-create the quilt I made, or you can use them to plan your own.

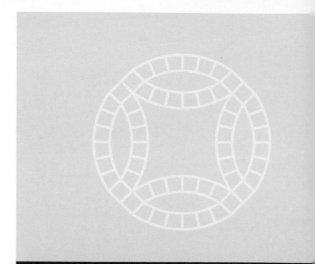

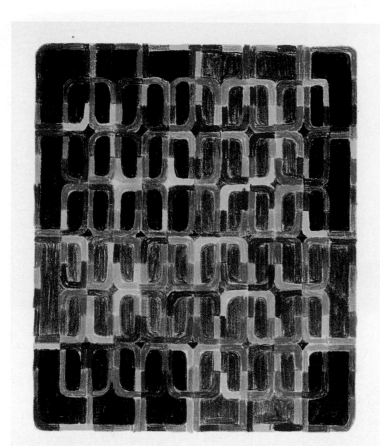

The first design contained an elongated-block design.

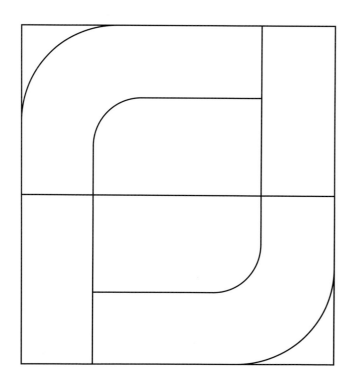

A square block was selected for the final design.

AN EVER-FIXED MARK
patterns

Add seam allowance to all pieces.

Cutting instructions

For each block, cut two
A, B, C, and D pieces.

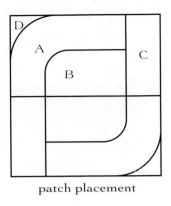

patch placement

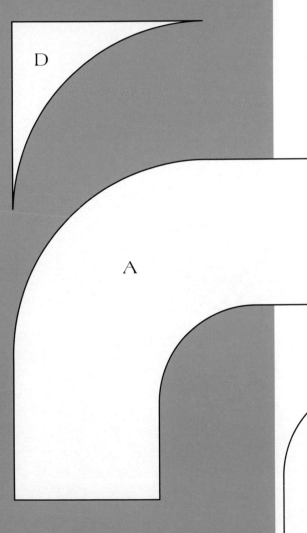

C

D

A

B

Marilyn Henrion

LEPRECHAUN WEDDING

72" x 84", Cottons
Machine pieced & hand quilted

Deanna Deason Dison

I was afraid I wouldn't have time to make a Double Wedding Ring, but I decided to try. I finished it in six weeks!

Deanna Deason Dison Spearsville, LA

MY QUILTMAKING

As a teenager, I helped my mother make quilts, and once married, I made them for use. But I'm actually very much an outdoors person. In college, I studied landscape design, and later completed an M.A. in botany. I opened a flower shop and later a greenhouse, where I raised foliage plants until 1988.

I live in the country and spend much time working in the yard. People who know me are sometimes surprised to discover that I spend a lot of time sitting inside at a sewing machine. Presently, I help my auctioneer husband on Saturdays, and the rest of the time I am able to quilt.

I go to every class, lecture, and quilt show I can, and I also spend much time reading books to keep up with new developments in the field. There is always something to learn.

MY QUILT

I made a traditional Double Wedding Ring scrap quilt for my daughter when she married in 1978, and in 1988, I made a Pickle Dish. With LEPRECHAUN WEDDING I wanted to work with the Double Wedding Ring pattern in a less traditional way.

I drew the quilt until it was just what I wanted. Then I had copies made and colored them in. While I was coloring, my very active four-year-old granddaughter talked on and on about a leprechaun. Another of my granddaughters had passed away in 1992, so my quilts made during that period had been sad. My four-year-old granddaughter's activity lifted my spirits, and this quilt became a happier project.

The quilt was a challenge to construct. I had the 4" and 8" blocks all laid out on the bed when my kittens got on the bed and scrambled everything. It took another three hours to lay it out again.

Looking at the quilt now, it's not a sad quilt, but it was made during the saddest part of my life.

MY DESIGN

This design was the end result of an extensive series of sketches, as shown below and on page 14.

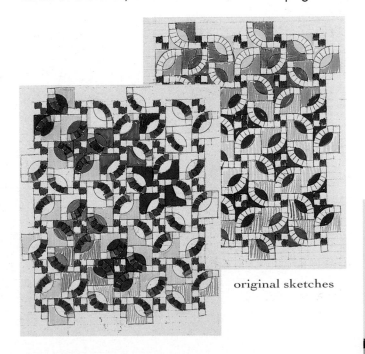

original sketches

more sketches

LEPRECHAUN WEDDING
block designs

This quilt was developed from the three blocks shown on page 15. Use this grid to plan your own quilt based on this design. See pages 16–17 for full-sized templates.

Enlarge grid as desired for planning your quilt.

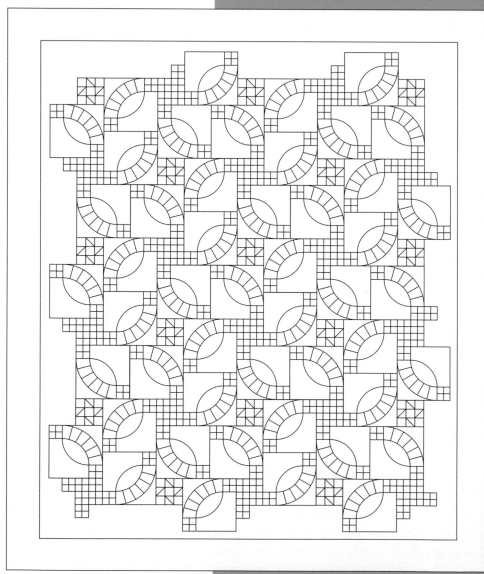

E yellow	E black	E yellow	E black
E black	E yellow	E black	E yellow
E yellow	E black	E yellow	E black
E black	E yellow	E black	E yellow

G dk blue	F dk blue / F gold	G dk blue
F dk blue / F gold	G gold	F gold / F dk blue
G dk blue	F gold / F dk blue	G dk blue

color placement

See full-size patterns on pages 16 and 17.

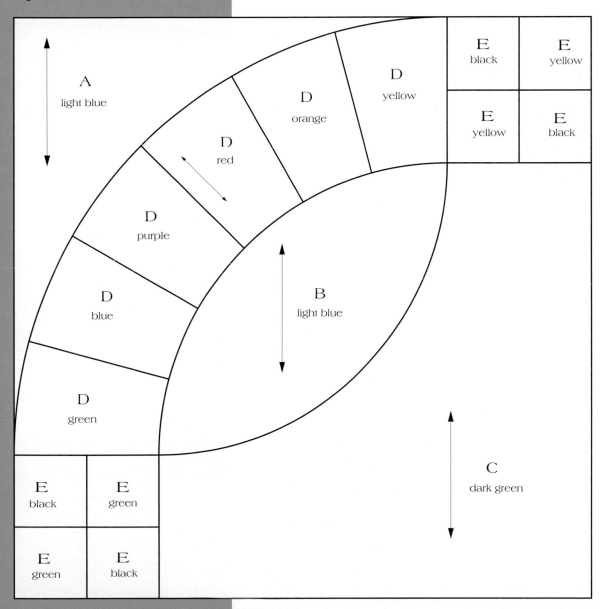

A
light blue

D yellow

E black | E yellow
E yellow | E black

D orange

D red

D purple

B light blue

D blue

D green

E black | E green
E green | E black

C
dark green

Deanna Deason Dison

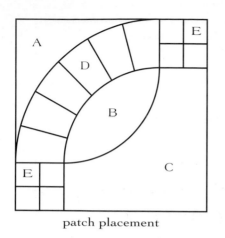

patch placement

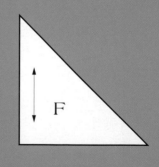

patch placement

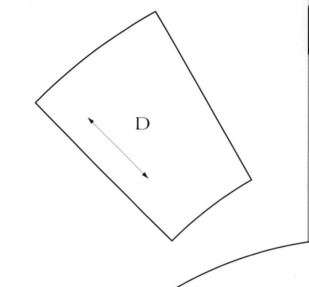

D

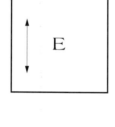

E

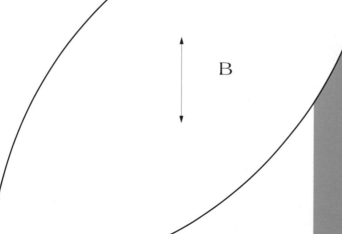

B

F

G

Double Wedding Ring

Deanna Deason Dison

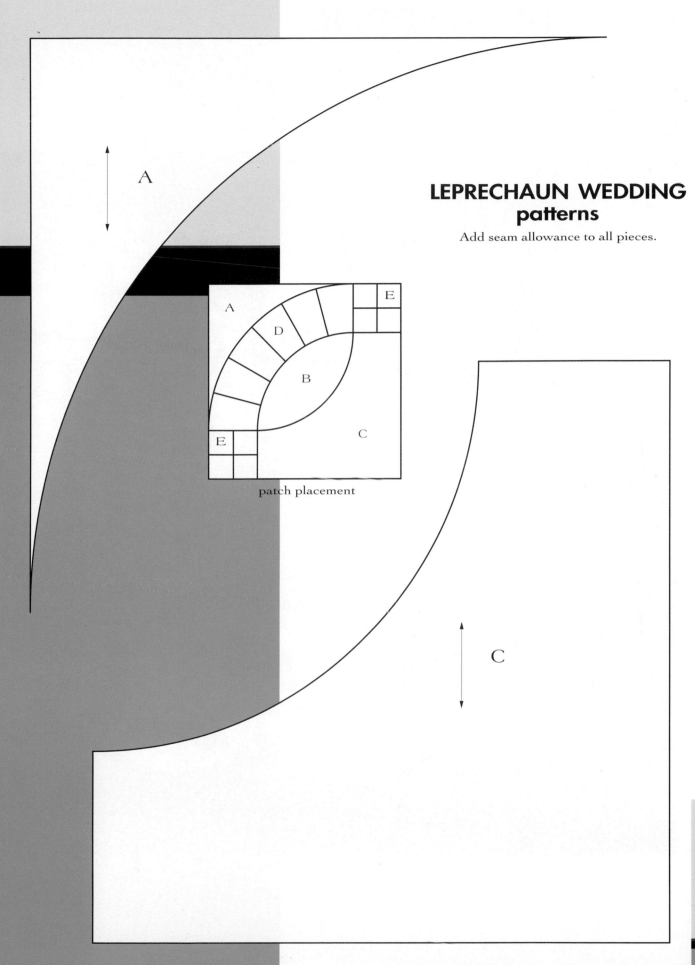

LEPRECHAUN WEDDING
patterns

Add seam allowance to all pieces.

A

patch placement

C

SHOTGUN WEDDNG

52" x 53", Cottons, cotton blends,
crossing-guard fabric
Machine pieced & quilted

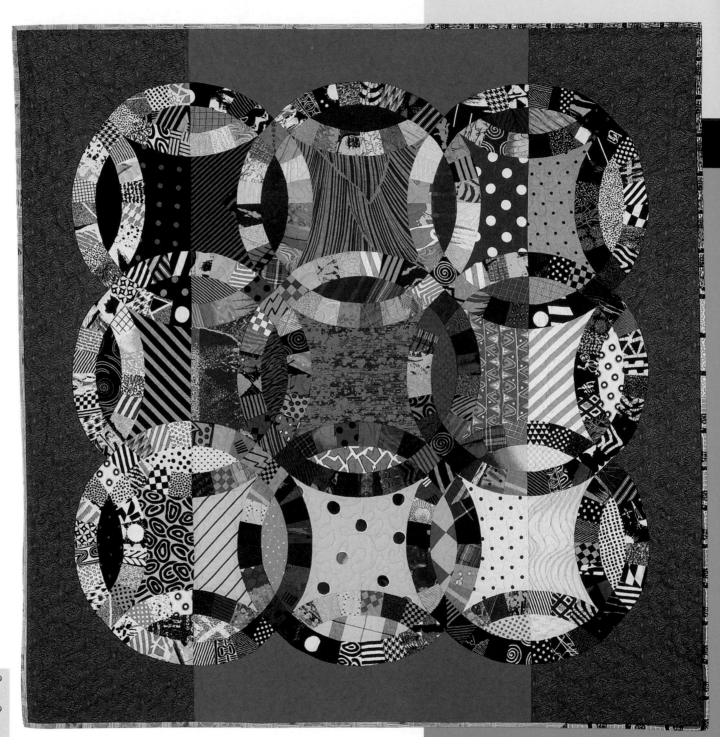

Marion Ongerth

Marion Ongerth

Berkeley, CA

*The title "Shotgun Wedding"
came from nowhere —
the outrageous orange just looked
as if it had needed
to be forced into the quilt.*

MY QUILTMAKING

In 1981, I saw examples of student work from Roberta Horton's Amish class on the walls of a fabric store. I was immediately attracted to the bright colors and geometric shapes. It was my first exposure to the quilt as an art medium. Not being from a quilting background, I had a lot of skills to learn and took many classes before I began to work on original designs.

I studied graphic design in college, and my primary interest is in manipulating color to heighten its tension and emotional impact. My inspiration comes from many sources, including the works of the French impressionist painters and American blues and jazz improvisation. I design my quilts to be viewed vertically on the wall rather than horizontally on a bed.

Working with fabric is essential to me. We are wrapped in cloth at birth, live our lives surrounded by cloth, and are finally wrapped in cloth at death. By making my art in this medium, I feel connected to something timeless and enduring.

MY QUILT

When I think of the Double Wedding Ring pattern, I think of a white background with rings of 1930s house-dress fabrics. I wanted my quilt to reflect the variety of fabrics available in the 1990s. I wanted it to be a record of my fabric collection.

For many years, I have been working with the circle motif, the symbol of wholeness and the self. I wanted to honor the quilting tradition that inspired

my art by designing a piece that married the traditional Double Wedding Ring pattern with the strong colors I love.

I challenge myself by posing color problems and finding solutions for them. I'm fascinated by the interplay of richly mixed colors that produce both emotional reaction and a rhythmic riot of colorful movement.

I designed my piece without much thought to background fabric, and the challenge for me was to find one that was assertive enough to stand up to the strong colors in the rings. I solved my problem by using an orange polyester crossing-guard fabric, the only orange I could find strong enough to balance the turquoise.

ROYAL WEDDING

84" x 100", Cottons
Hand & machine pieced, hand quilted

Pieceful Scrappers Willowdale, Ontario, Canada

OUR QUILTMAKING

We began quilting together in 1986. There are now seven of us, and we all belong to the York Heritage Guild, a large quilt guild in Toronto with over 400 members. Two of our members were charter members of that guild.

Drawn together by our mutual love of scrap quilts and the pleasure of working together on a large quilt frame, we meet every Wednesday to hand piece and hand quilt scrap quilts. I joined the group last, and have been quilting since 1985. Most members have been quilting for 10 to 12 years.

We select a pattern, determine the number of blocks each member must do, and then all make our own blocks, using our own fabrics. Usually, there is one coordinating fabric we all use. Sometimes our quilts include bright colors or a dark background, but generally we tend to be pretty traditional.

OUR QUILT

Competition wasn't really our goal when we started this quilt, but we have had much local success, so we have tried to make each quilt a little more interesting, a little better than the last. This quilt is made in a pattern we call Royal Wedding.

This design was based on a traditional block for which a pattern was given in *Scraps Can Be Beautiful* by Jan Halgrimson (1979, Weaver-Finch Publications). We modified the pattern given for the traditional block, which was called Chimney Swal-

lows in that book and Coronation in Jinny Beyer's. Names with royal suggestions prompted our title for the modified block drafted by member Mary Lou Watson.

We had reservations about using this pattern because it was quite a challenge to piece. Some of us liked the challenge. Others weren't too crazy about it. We were rewarded when we saw the quilt put together.

We had already started this quilt when we heard of the museum's competition, and we felt this design would be perfect.

ROYAL WEDDING BLOCK

Pieces D, Dr, and E are so similar, we found it necessary to mark each template with a small circle to indicate the end farthest from the middle of the block.

Within the seam allowance on the fabric pieces, we marked the identifying letter of that piece as well as the small circle. We redrafted G in order to eliminate the seam between blocks. G pieces were stitched in place after all the centers were pieced.

Double Wedding Ring

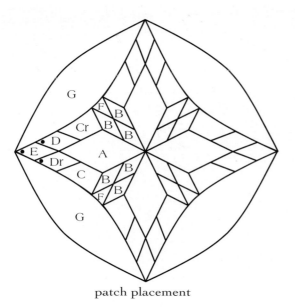

patch placement

This block is developed from the traditional Chimney Swallows block, as shown in *Scraps Can Be Beautiful* by Jan Halgrimson (Weaver-Finch Publications)

Enlarge grid as desired for planning your quilt

ROYAL WEDDING
patterns
12" block
Add seam allowance to all pieces.

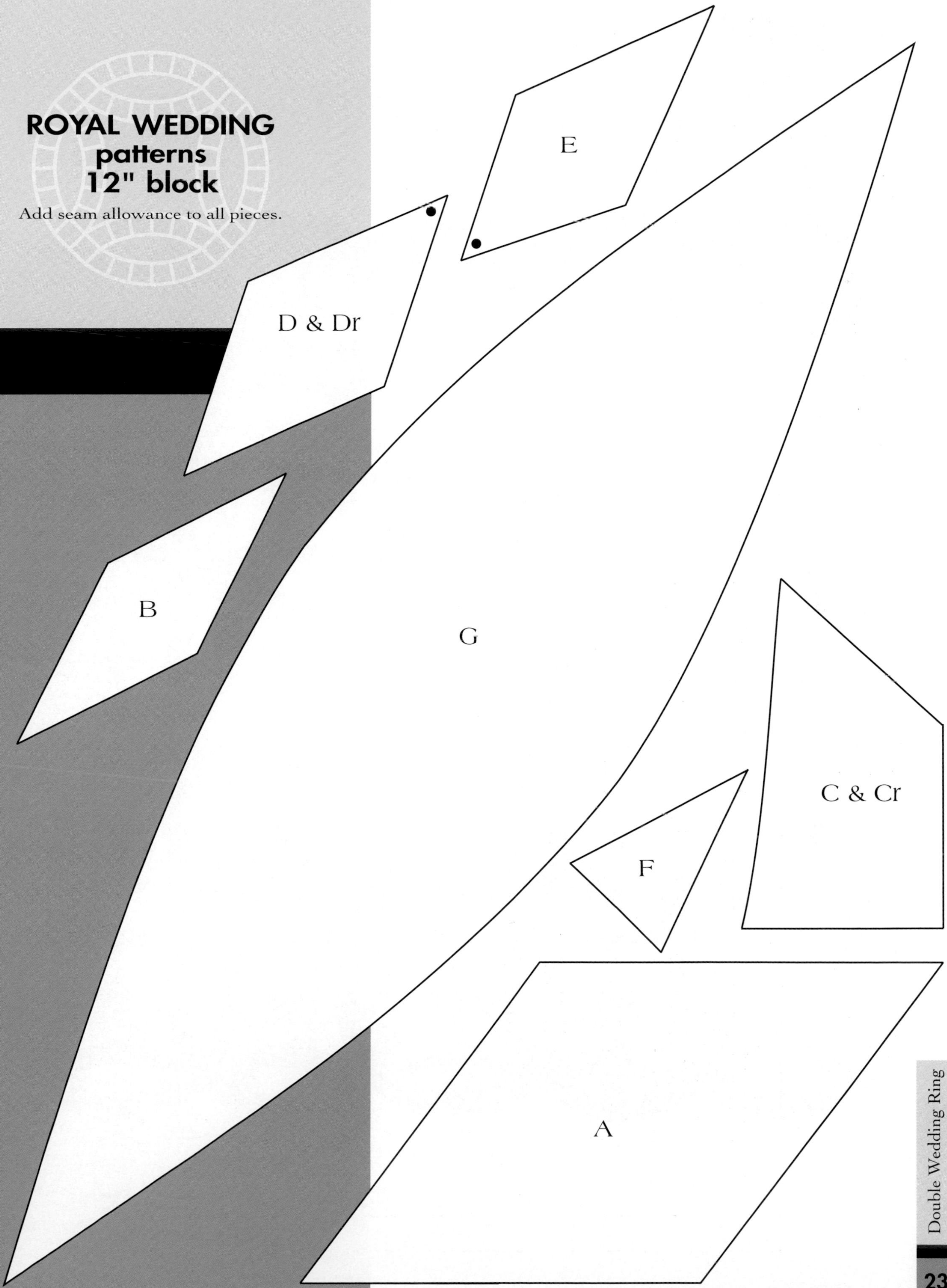

E

D & Dr

B

G

C & Cr

F

A

MEDLEY

63" x 63", Cottons
Machine pieced & quilted

Elsie Vredenburg

Elsie Vredenburg

Tustin, MI

MY QUILTMAKING

My grandmother lived with us when I was in high school. She had pieced quilts all of her life, and one day announced that she and I were going to make a quilt. I had taken sewing in home economics, but wasn't overly enthusiastic about learning to quilt. My mother encouraged me to do it because Grandma needed to be needed; she was used to being busy. I filled the gap and got hooked on quilting. I didn't do much while my children were small, but the U.S. Bicentennial brought me back to quilting. I made a small wallhanging to commemorate the event.

There is something in me that needs to create. I don't have an art background and hate to use the word artist, but there is an artist hidden in me that is trying to get out. It is the visual element of quilting that interests me most. I am visually attracted to quilts.

MY QUILT

I've made lots of Double Wedding Ring quilts. In fact, the third quilt I ever made was a Double Wedding Ring, probably because my grandma had the pattern and it intrigued me. It's also a good quilt for using up little scraps. Almost every time I make one I say I will never make another. The pattern doesn't have the nice straight seams I like to work with. It's more challenging to get the quilt to lie flat.

Just before beginning this quilt I was working on another quilt in which I wanted to include some of my grandmother's patterns. One of these patterns was the Double Wedding Ring, but I didn't want to include any curves. As I tried to develop that pattern using angles rather than curves, I suddenly realized I could make a quilt for the MAQS contest.

I designed this block with no curved seams using the Electric Quilt® program, a computer program I've been working with for a year. The quilt is made of blocks that are square, and the background makes a second circle. Study is needed to understand how it went together.

FABRICS

I used assorted scraps of pastel green, blue, pink, and lavender for the background rings (templates A,C,D,F,G,I), and dark jewel tones for the foreground rings (templates B,E,H), teal and purple for the pinwheels (template K), and a lighter teal and fuchsia for the stars (template J). All templates need to be reversed for the opposite half of the block.

For each 12" block, cut eight (half in reverse) of each template. See photo of quilt for possible fabric placement. (Exception: the last row of blocks has six of each template, in order to make the scalloped edge).

Stitch together in rows:
Row 1: A, B, C
Row 2: D, E, F
Row 3: G, H, I, J

Stitch rows together, adding K to ABC row. This will give you a right-angle triangle. Using the reverse pieces, stitch the other half of the block. Stitch the two triangles together to form a square. This is one-fourth of the block. Stitch the other three-fourths in the same manner. Join the four sections together, with J pieces forming a pinwheel in the center of the block.

QUILTING

I machine quilted the background in the ditch with invisible thread, the rings with two colors of metallic thread and a twin needle in a freehand cable design, and the stars in gold metallic thread in a four-petal design.

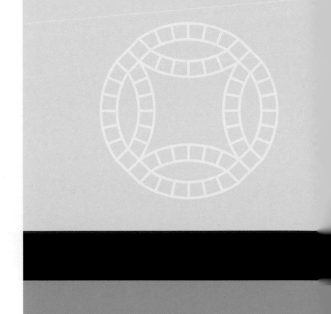

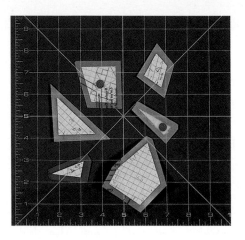

A star forms where four blocks meet.

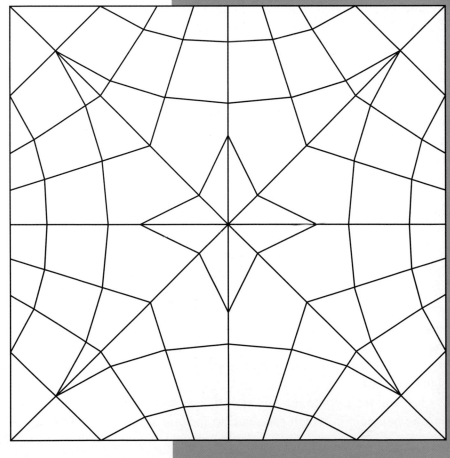

Elsie Vredenburg

MEDLEY patterns

Add seam allowance to all pieces.

[P]ress: Left up, right down, center open.
[O]n rings: Center row out, end rows in.

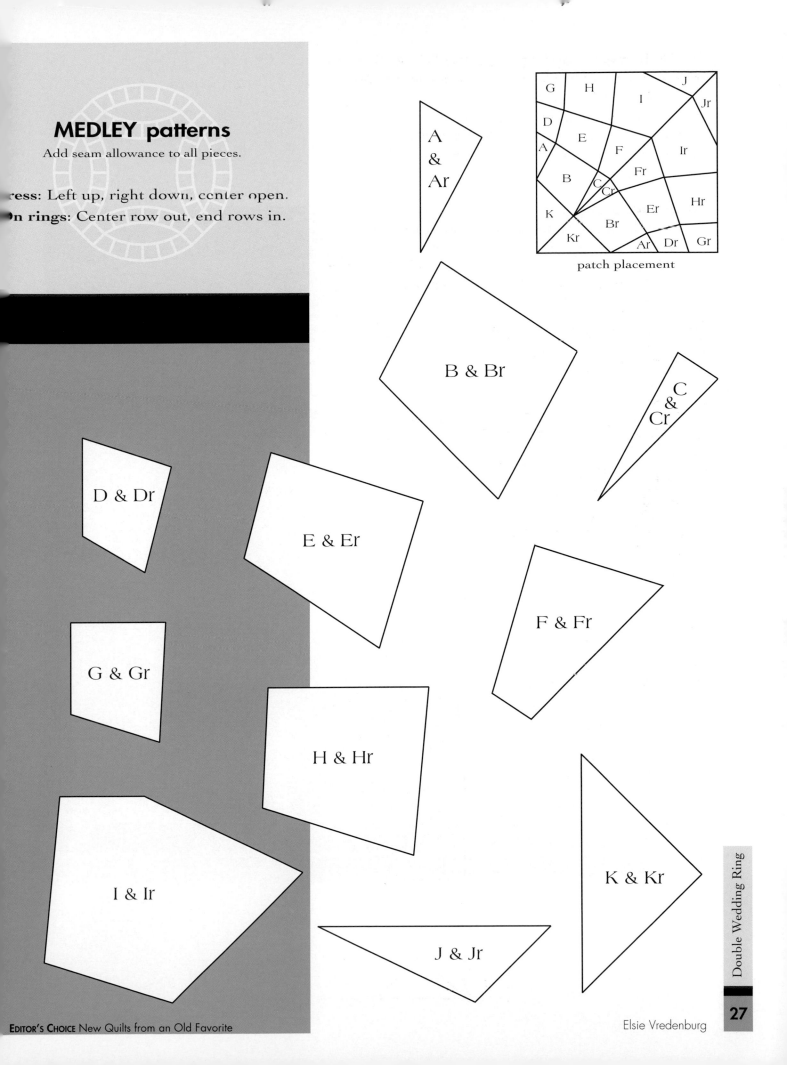

patch placement

A & Ar

B & Br

C & Cr

D & Dr

E & Er

F & Fr

G & Gr

H & Hr

I & Ir

J & Jr

K & Kr

AGONY AND ECSTASY

53¼" x 53¼", Cottons
Machine pieced & quilted

28

Shirley Robinson Davis

EDITOR'S CHOICE New Quilts from an Old Favorite

Shirley Robinson Davis · Prescott, AZ

MY QUILTMAKING

I was a professional rodeo photographer, but when we moved, I was suddenly too far away from my work to continue. My sister-in-law suggested I take a quilting class, and reluctantly I did. I immediately "got hooked" and have abandoned photography completely. Relocated in Arizona, I taught in a shop for a period. I like to design and make controlled but original art quilts.

I like machine quilting because it allows me to get quilts done – my machine is a best friend. I really enjoy looking at hand quilting, but my attention span just doesn't last long enough for me to hand quilt my work.

My husband is surprised I have stuck with quilting so long. I tend to jump around with many things, but I have so many fabrics, I will probably have to stick with this.

MY QUILT

When I left Nevada, the quilt shop owners there gave me John Flynn's patterns. With our 40th anniversary coming up, I decided a Double Wedding Ring quilt would be a good present for my husband. In making that Southwestern theme Double Wedding Ring quilt, I found John Flynn's method so easy that I had no hesitation about making another quilt in this pattern.

When I began AGONY AND ECSTASY, I knew I didn't want an ordinary ring. I wanted it shaded. With no particular design in mind, I just started cutting fabric and putting it on my design wall. I cut pieces of hand-dyed sueded cottons from Cherrywood Quilts & Fabrics®, put them on the wall, stood back, and squinted. If the design didn't thrill me, I knew the piece wouldn't work.

The title came about because the quilt was such agony to make – I just kept cutting fabrics. I worked until the last minute. My good friend Sharon, who is also in the exhibit, kept me working. If it hadn't been for her, I might never have finished.

CURVED PIECING

Use the following method to get a perfect fit on curved pieces:

• Fold the pieces in half and finger press at the center of the seam line. If desired also clip ⅛" into seam allowance or dot with a pencil mark at that point.

• Clip ⅛" into the seam allowance of the concave piece only, along the entire curve (Fig. 1 on the following page).

• Place the concave (inside clipped piece) on top of the convex (outward curve) piece, matching center marks. Pin, starting in the center, matching ends, and then pinning in between (Fig. 2).

• Sew with the concave piece on top, removing pins as you come to them. If you spread your hand on the piece and rotate the fabric in one continuous motion as you sew, it will be easy to get a smooth seam (Fig. 3).

Double Wedding Ring

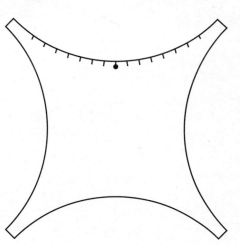

Fig. 1

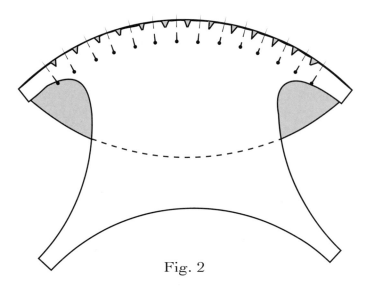

Fig. 2

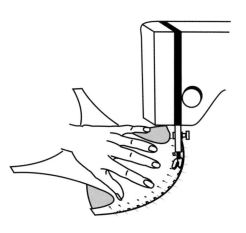

Fig. 3

Close-up of AGONY AND ECSTASY.

Shirley Robinson Davis

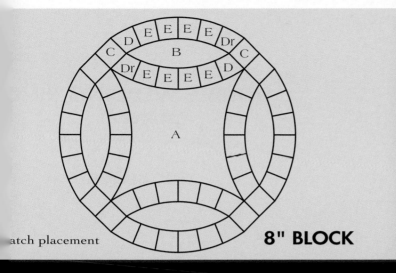

match placement

8" BLOCK

DOUBLE WEDDING RING
patterns

Add seam allowance to all pieces.

Included in this section are four different sizes of full templates for the traditional Double Wedding Ring pattern. Select the size most appropriate for your project.

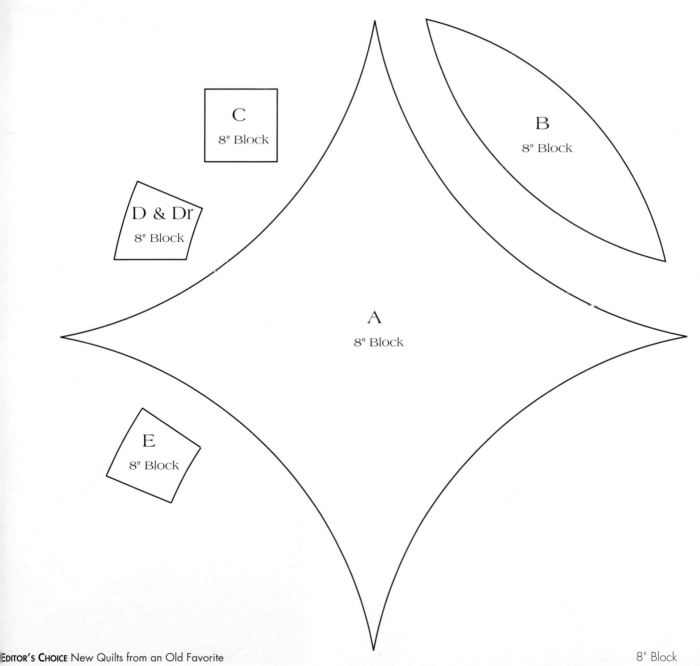

C
8" Block

B
8" Block

D & Dr
8" Block

A
8" Block

E
8" Block

Double Wedding Ring

C D E E E E Dr C
C   B   Dr   C
Dr E E E E D

A

patch placement

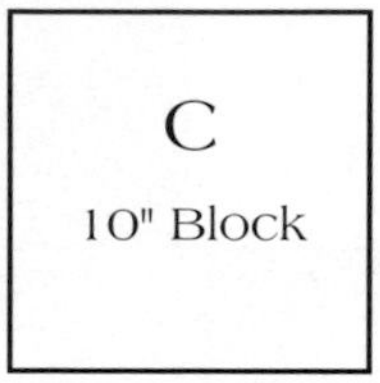

DOUBLE WEDDING RIN
patterns
Add seam allowance to all pieces.

10" BLOCK

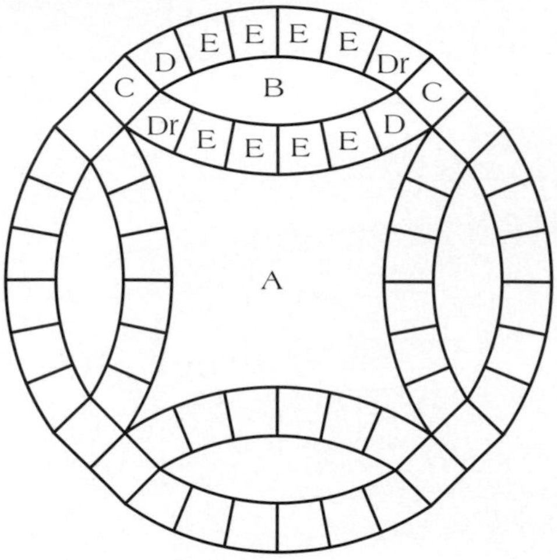

C
10" Block

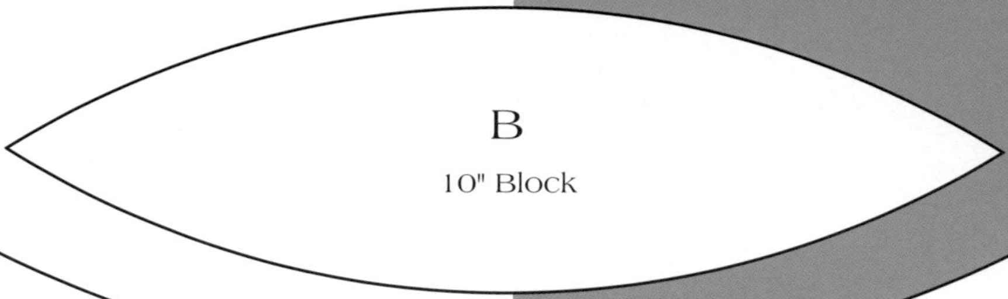

B
10" Block

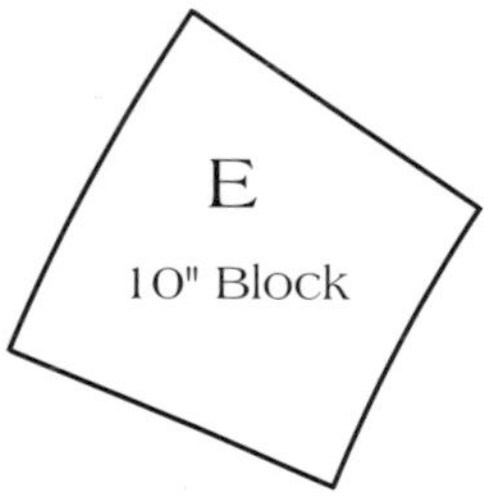

E
10" Block

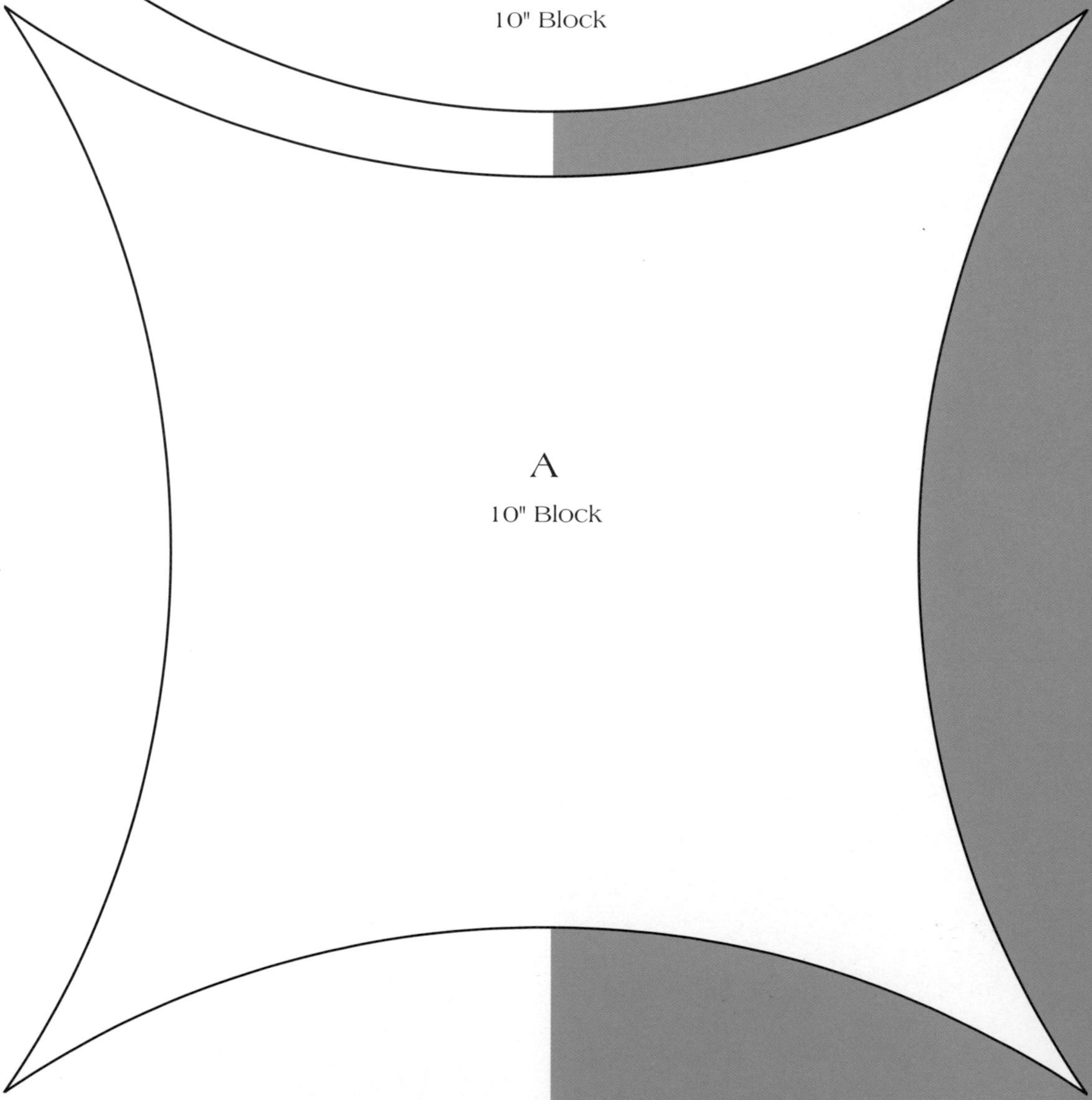

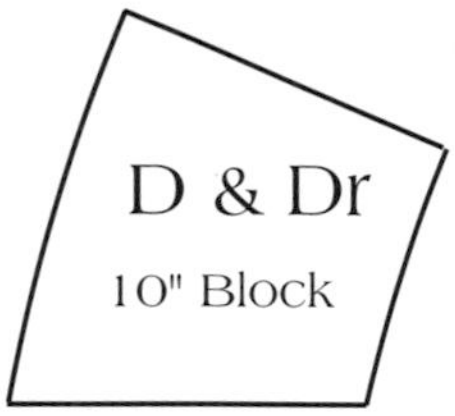

D & Dr
10" Block

A
10" Block

DOUBLE WEDDING RING
patterns

Add seam allowance to all pieces.

12" BLOCK

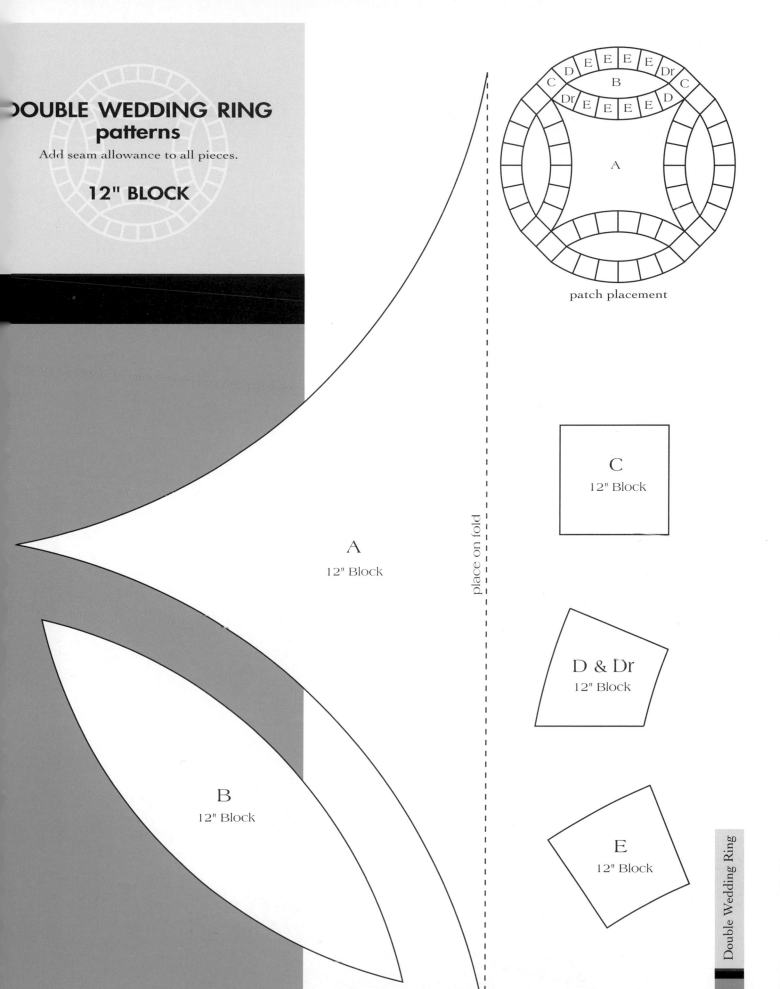

patch placement

A
12" Block

place on fold

B
12" Block

C
12" Block

D & Dr
12" Block

E
12" Block

12" Block

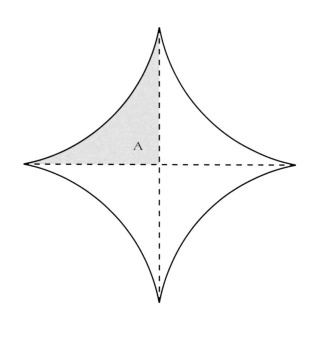

Enlarge grid as desired for planning your quilt.

DOUBLE WEDDING RING
patterns
Add seam allowance to all pieces.

14" BLOCK

A

A

14" Block
(one quarter of piece)

14" Block

DOUBLE WEDDING RING
patterns

Add seam allowance to all pieces.

14" BLOCK

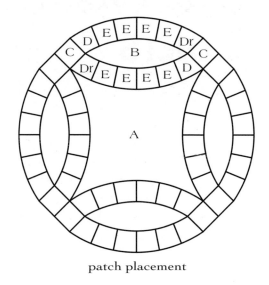

patch placement

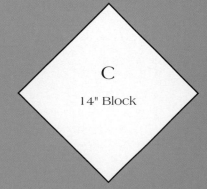

B

14" Block

C

14" Block

D & Dr

14" Block

E

14" Block

LOG CABIN QUILTS

The Log Cabin pattern, with its narrow interlocking "logs," has long been a favorite with quiltmakers. It is likely that the pattern was developed with an eye to using up narrow strips and other fabric scraps not suitable for cutting squares and triangles.

There are several variations of the Log Cabin block. In the traditional block, the logs are sewn on in a clockwise or counterclockwise spiral. The block is divided in half diagonally, with dark fabrics in one half and light fabric in the other. When these blocks are set side by side, many interesting settings can be created, depending on how the blocks are turned. Traditional Log Cabin quilt settings include Barn Raising, Straight Furrow, Sunshine and Shadow, and Zigzag (see page 62 for examples).

In the Courthouse Steps block variation, the logs are added to opposite rather than adjacent sides, and in the Chimneys and Cornerstones variation, little squares march diagonally through the center of the block.

The block can be further changed by varying the width of the logs and the size of the center square. Several interesting possibilities can be developed by moving the center square off-center.

Another Log Cabin variation, the Pineapple block, has diagonal rows of logs in addition to the horizontal and vertical ones. (See QUASARS, page 42, and SPELLBOUND, page 50.)

Piecing patterns and a foundation pattern are provided to help you create your own beautiful Log Cabin quilt.

LOG CABIN SQUARED

75" x 75", Cottons
Machine pieced on paper foundation blocks &
machine quilted by Fran McEachem

37

Nancy Taylor

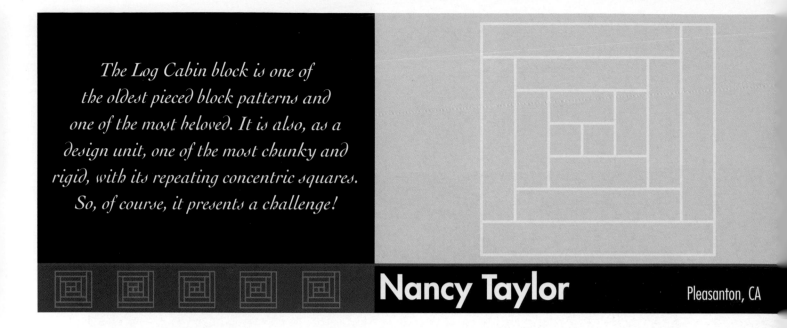

The Log Cabin block is one of the oldest pieced block patterns and one of the most beloved. It is also, as a design unit, one of the most chunky and rigid, with its repeating concentric squares. So, of course, it presents a challenge!

Nancy Taylor

Pleasanton, CA

MY QUILTMAKING

I made my first quilt in 1975, for my then five-year-old daughter's bed. I would have to say that my mother, Margaret Vantine, had some responsibility for my becoming a quilter since we became quilters together through the making of this quilt. Neither one of us had ever made a quilt, but she offered to quilt it if I pieced and appliquéd it, so we learned together.

Today, my mother still quilts some of my quilts with the tiniest, most beautiful stitches. My oldest daughter, for whom the quilt was made, has since learned to quilt and produce tiny, even stitches too. This skill has skipped a generation. I remain in awe of both of them.

In addition to making quilts, for eight years I was co-owner of Going to Pieces, a quilt shop in Pleasanton, California. I have recently been creating my own fabric designs for my quilts, using fabric dyes. I spray, paint, immersion dye, and use wax resist to create patterning. I enjoy this aspect and will be concentrating my energies on producing quilts that are completely my own expression.

MY QUILT

This quilt was inspired by a black and white photograph of an antique quilt with blocks set on point. This set offered strong graphic possibilities for a contemporary version of a very traditional pattern. I have made two other Log Cabin quilts, each time motivated by the desire to create something different with this rather chunky design unit.

This time I decided to let the entire quilt echo the individual block design of concentric squares. I will probably be drawn to the Log Cabin again by the challenge it presents.

This quilt was made with and for the joy of working with color. I liked modulating and adjusting each color within its own band, and working with prints that added visual texture, an element second only in importance to color.

I was pleased with the resulting integration of strong graphic design and color. This quilt hangs on my living room wall, and I am energized when I walk in and feel its radiating color.

LOG CABIN SQUARED

The block I used has ¾" logs, is 6¾" finished, and is 7¼" with seam allowances. To draw the paper foundation, draw the block on accurate graph paper, as seen when finished (with seam lines drawn, rather than seam allowance edges). Extend the log outlines or seam lines ¼" above and below their intersections. Indicate on the pattern by shading which logs are dark. Draw a star in the center square. (See page 41 for my full-size pattern.)

Print the pattern on a copier. Two blocks will fit snugly on an 8½" x 14" sheet; you can cut the blocks apart to use them. Make sure the copier that you choose will not distort the image in either direction. Superimpose the original onto the copy, then hold it up to a light to compare the two outlines. Cut fabric strips across the width of fabric

Log Cabin

which has been folded in fourths. Cut strips ⅛" wider than the usual width desired. The logs in my pattern are ¾" wide finished. Ordinarily, they would be cut 1¼" wide including seam allowances. If an extra ⅛" is added, making the cut strips 1⅜" wide, there are fewer problems when sewing from the opposite side of a paper pattern.

The strips of fabric are stacked side by side in two rows. One row contains light fabrics, the other row darker fabrics. I compose each block before I sew by selecting which fabric I want to use for each side – dark and light. I cut two 1⅜" squares, one dark for the center and one light for the first log. Then, with the help of a paper that is marked with the length of each successive log, I cut each fabric strip slightly longer than the length indicated on my chart. I lay the logs out in the order in which they will be sewn.

All sewing is done on the lines on the paper pattern, but all fabrics are arranged on the reverse side of the paper. To begin the block, place a 1⅜" light square face down on a 1⅜" dark square, which will be the center square of the block. Hold the paper pattern up to a light source, with the Log Cabin design facing you. Put the two squares on the back of the paper with the wrong side of the dark fabric against the paper. Center the shadow of the squares directly over the starred center square on the pattern and distribute the seam allowance evenly around the marked square. Using a fine pin, pin through the paper of the starred square to hold the fabric pieces in place for sewing.

Before sewing, place a larger, new, sharp sewing machine needle in your machine. I use a 14/90.

Set your machine for smaller stitches. My machine is usually set at around a 2 or 2½ stitch length. For sewing on a paper foundation, I reduce the length to 1½.

By using a larger needle and taking stitches that are closer together, the eventual paper removal is much easier.

With the fabric pieces in place on the wrong side of the foundation pattern, place the paper pattern under the presser foot, face up, with the fabric pieces underneath. Starting ¼" above the seam line, sew along the line indicated between the dark square and the light square on your pattern. When finished, cut the threads, remove the pins, and turn the paper over. Fold the top square right side out, finger press, then press the seam lightly with a dry iron.

Place a large piece of muslin on top of your ironing surface. The photocopy ink will often transfer to your ironing board since you will be pressing with the copy side down. After pressing, place the next fabric strip face down over the first two fabrics. Again, hold the paper up to a light source, fabric side facing away from you. Align the shadow of the fabric strip with its seam allowance extending ¼" outside the photocopied seam line. Pin in place, with the pin parallel to the seam line, in the center of the strip. Sew as before, beginning and ending ¼" above and below the intersecting seam line. As logs get longer, it may be necessary to pin at the top and bottom of each log. Cut the end of each strip to fit by folding it back against itself ¼" above the seam line and trimming carefully with scissors.

When the block is complete, press well. Trim by rotary cutting ¼" outside the block outline all around the pattern.

Remove the paper from each outside perimeter log. The remaining paper can be removed after the blocks are sewn together.

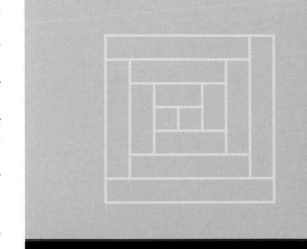

Close-up of LOG CABIN SQUARED

Log Cabin

Nancy Taylor

LOG CABIN SQUARED
foundation pattern
shown at 100%

Lines represent seam lines, not fabric edges.

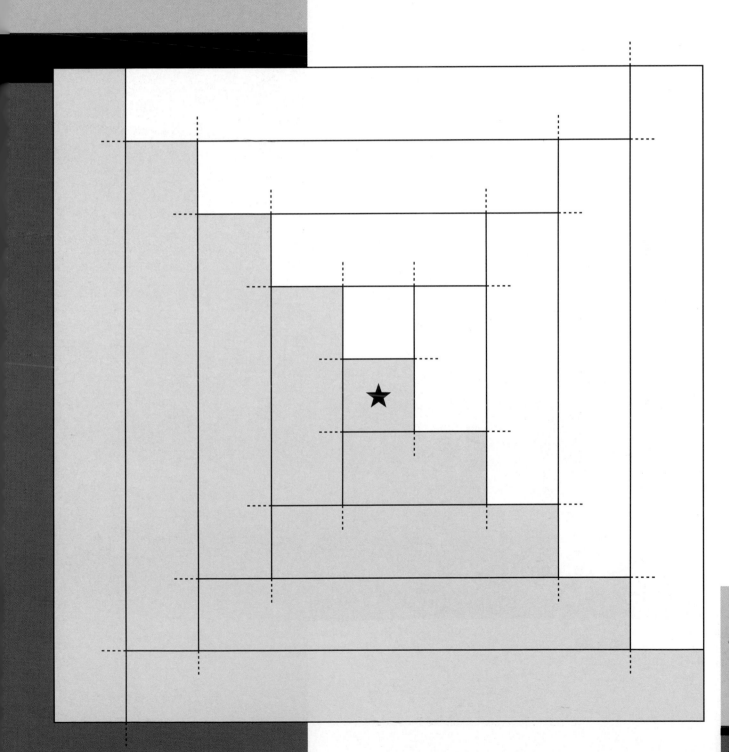

Nancy Taylor

QUASARS

61" x 61", Cottons, including dyed & air brushed, many by Debra Lunn, rayon & monofilament thread. Machine pieced on foundation blocks, machine quilted

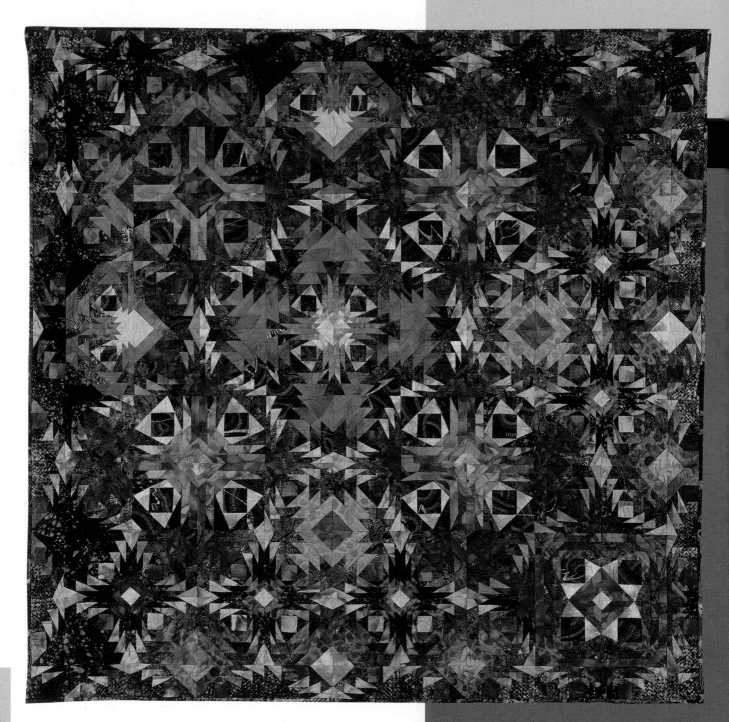

Log Cabin

42

Laura Murray

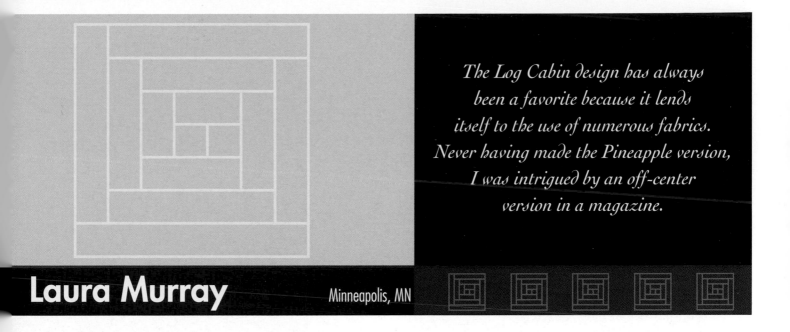

Laura Murray

Minneapolis, MN

MY QUILTMAKING

Though I have a long history of needlework, I have never been attracted to traditional quiltmaking. But in 1989, to make my daughter the bed quilt she wanted, I took a class. Soon after, I visited the art building at the 1989 Minnesota State Fair where Wendy Richardson's quilt NOT QUITE BLACK AND WHITE was displayed. This first "in the cloth" view of a non-traditional quilt opened my eyes to wondrous possibilities.

I knew I had found my perfect form of creative self-expression. It had never occurred to me that I could create my own designs for my needlework. Once I discovered contemporary quilts, I became completely hooked. Not a day has gone by since my first class that I have not been engaged in some way with quiltmaking.

I am currently working on a pictorial Art Nouveau design and am learning to produce my own original fabrics in addition to collecting unusual textiles from around the world. I really can't tell you exactly where it is all headed. It's the process of "pushing the edges" of my own development that is important to me.

MY QUILT

I prefer working directly with fabric color and texture, so I drafted the two basic blocks and then sewed four identical blocks to form a set. The rest of the design grew around that unit. In the past, I've used the Log Cabin for family quilts meant to be used on a bed. This is the first time I've used it for an art quilt, a quilt which requires more attention to detail and design and which is meant to hang on the wall.

QUASARS involves more discipline and structure than my work usually does. Several days after I began the design, my daughter's neck was fractured in a swimming pool accident. She is now completely recovered, but for three months, there were many unknowns. I found the process of working with small pieces, one unit at a time, and then juxtaposing them with other pieces very soothing. I lacked the energy to be spontaneous. All I could handle was one piece at a time, building as I went. When my life is in order, my work is much more free-flowing and spontaneous. I usually have little interest in the structure or repetition of traditional geometric design.

QUASARS

Working with off-center versions of the Pineapple Log Cabin block, I created a set of four and then let the quilt develop from there. I basically worked with the three blocks shown on pages 44 and 45, rotating them and combining them in various ways. As you can see in the quilt photo, this design created with only three blocks looks very complex and offers great opportunities for experimenting with color. Try your own hand at achieving a variety of effects with these blocks.

Log Cabin

Close-up of QUASARS

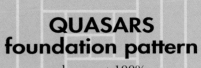

**QUASARS
foundation pattern**
shown at 100%

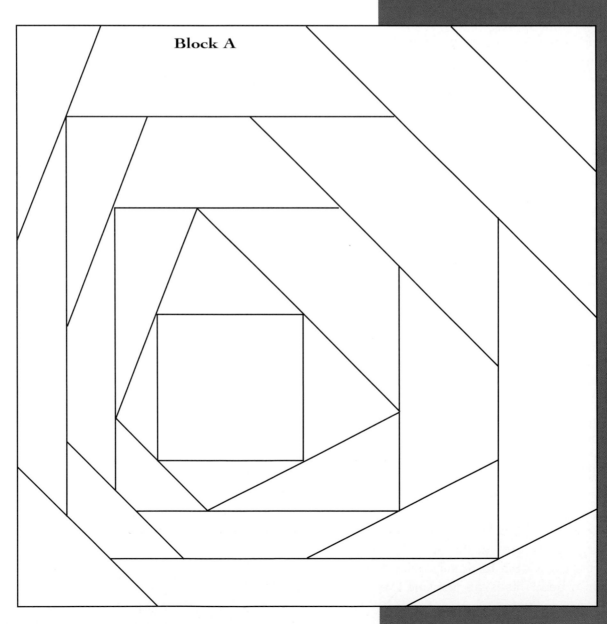

Block A

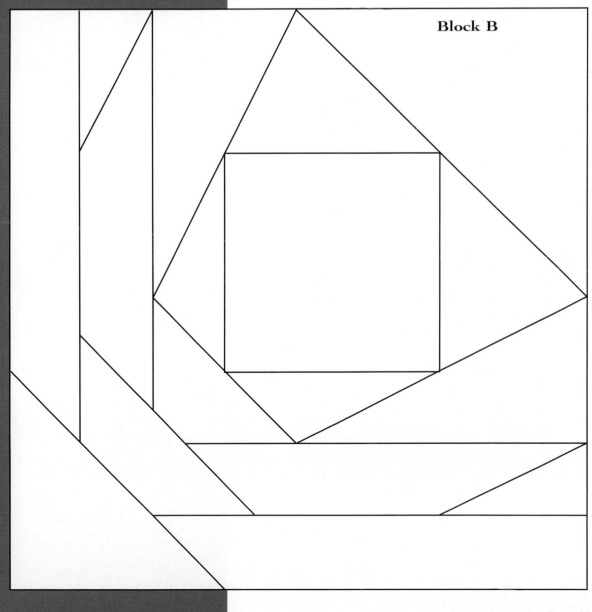

**QUASARS
foundation
patterns**

shown at 100%

Block C
(border)

Block B

Laura Murray

Log Cabin

SUPERNOVA 1994

50" x 50", Cottons
Machine pieced & quilted

Log Cabin

46

Barbara T. Kaempfer

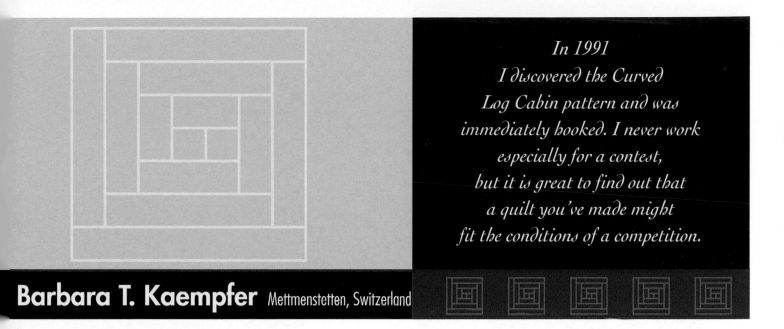

In 1991
I discovered the Curved
Log Cabin pattern and was
immediately hooked. I never work
especially for a contest,
but it is great to find out that
a quilt you've made might
fit the conditions of a competition.

Barbara T. Kaempfer Mettmenstetten, Switzerland

MY QUILTMAKING

I began quilting in 1982, just after I moved with my family from Switzerland to Raleigh, North Carolina, where my husband had been transferred for three years. At first it was quite difficult to adjust in a completely new environment. Luckily, there was another Swiss family in Raleigh. The first time we visited their home, Sonja, the wife, showed me the antique quilts she was collecting. Never having paid attention to quilts, I could not understand her excitement. I thought these quilts were pretty, but that was it.

In September Sonja asked me to attend a quilt class with her. Having always loved to sew and having made most of my clothing, I agreed. Quilting changed my life. I "caught the virus."

Quilting has become very important in my life: I'm happy when working on a quilt. A wonderful side effect has been the many wonderful people I have met through quilting.

In addition to making quilts, I am teaching classes, and there are many projects I would like to complete!

MY QUILT

When I begin a new quilt, I never know exactly how it will turn out. The risk of a new project is fun. I've been working with the curved Log Cabin technique for four years, rotating the shapes to create the illusion of curves. In this quilt I experimented with how this technique looks when applied with a traditional setting like Barn Raising. Each

block needed to be drawn individually because the uneven blocks are all different. The fabric was sewn directly on this drawing, by machine, and the quilt was then machine quilted. I started in the center of the Barn Raising, working my way around. By using white fabric on the outermost strip of some of the blocks, stars emerged. My husband came up with the name SUPERNOVA. He thinks the red star amongst the other stars in the night sky shows the explosion of a star which is called Supernova. Often family members or friends are the ones who name my quilts.

There are so many more possibilities for curved Log Cabin quilts that I think I'll work with the pattern for some time to come.

SUPERNOVA

This quilt is a construction of uneven blocks. Every block has different angles on each corner and the side length differs, too. To construct such a quilt, one has to draw the whole quilt in its original size.

Printing the original design for this quilt, which includes 100 different blocks, was impossible, but the design can also be done with even blocks. To make a quilt similar to SUPERNOVA (but with even blocks), one can use an even block with 5" sides.

The 5" block on page 49 can be copied and used as a foundation sheet for as many blocks as you need. To make a quilt the size of SUPERNOVA, you would use 100 blocks.

Log Cabin

The fabric is sewn directly onto the paper foundation. It is very important to keep in mind that the resulting blocks will be a mirror image of the design. If the design for the final quilt shows blocks with a clockwise twist, the paper foundation needs to be drawn with a counterclockwise twist.

A center square with ¼" seam allowance is cut. The centerpiece is placed in such a way that it covers all the lines of the center on the paper foundation. Then the sewing is done from the center outward, using strips cut 1" wide. Before ironing, the seams are trimmed.

Using this block, you can make quilts with various traditional settings, such as Barn Raising, Straight Furrows, Light and Dark, and many more.

Straight Furrows layout.

Log Cabin

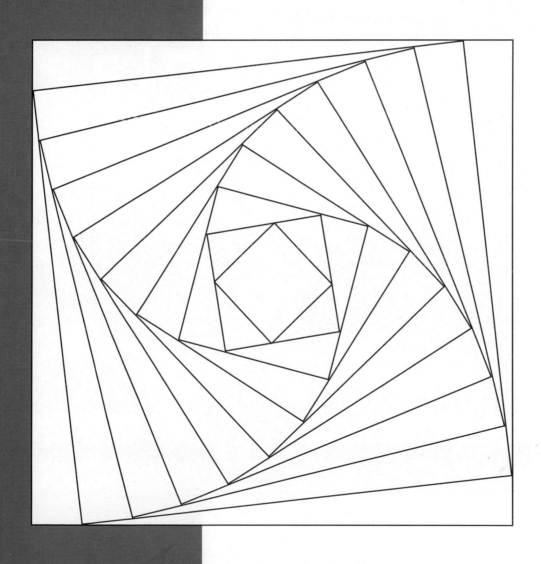

Log Cabin

SPELLBOUND

81" x 81", Cottons; some overdyed
Machine pieced on tear-away foun-
dation, hand quilted

Log Cabin

Allison Lockwood

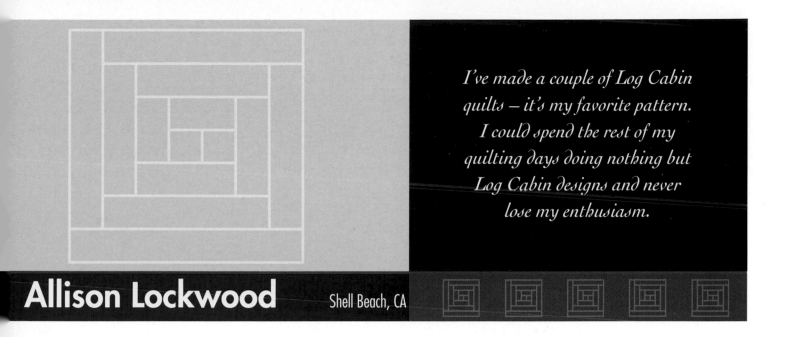

I've made a couple of Log Cabin quilts — it's my favorite pattern. I could spend the rest of my quilting days doing nothing but Log Cabin designs and never lose my enthusiasm.

Allison Lockwood
Shell Beach, CA

MY QUILTMAKING

I began quilting in 1986 after the birth of my second daughter. My former passion was ballet. As it became increasingly difficult to leave my young family to attend classes, I realized I had to give it up. To ease my disappointment, I signed up for a beginning patchwork class. I've traded one passion for another.

Currently, I make mostly large wall quilts that use a traditional block in an innovative way. I love to hand quilt and like to make quilting an important part of the design. My newest quilt mixes new fabrics, antique fabrics, and fabrics salvaged from thrift-store clothing.

I have three young daughters, so much of my quilting is done during the "guilt free" hours they're asleep. I have surprised myself in that I spend so many hours hand quilting. I find it to be very hypnotic.

My mother, June Alexis, is partially responsible for my becoming a quiltmaker. I was brought up by a mother who was and still is in a constant state of creative frenzy. She always encouraged artistic expression, so I can't imagine a life without some form of creative endeavor.

MY QUILT

I've spent many hours spellbound by the quilts in my large collection of books. I've especially been attracted to nineteenth century Pineapple Log Cabins. SPELLBOUND is an original design variation, made by using the traditional Pineapple Log

Cabin block, which has a very complex appearance. To learn how to piece one, I took a one-day class from Dixie Haywood. I started this quilt about a year later.

I made another Log Cabin quilt I call LAVISH MACTAVISH specifically to enter in the contest. After working on this quilt for over a year, I realized the quilt would not be finished in time for the entry deadline. Two weeks before the deadline, it dawned on me that SPELLBOUND might qualify. I'm glad I entered it!

The quilt is made from 81 identically constructed blocks. I'd like to experiment with designing other simple blocks. I don't feel very directed toward complicated piecing. I'm convinced that sometimes the simplest piecing can make the most fascinating quilts – if the fabric choices are exciting.

FOUNDATION PIECING

To design my quilt, I made several copies of the Pineapple block on a photocopier and then taped the blocks together. I used my children's crayons to color the blocks. After making three quilt designs, I chose my favorite, and that became my "map." I started making blocks from the center of the quilt and worked outward. My color choices were already made, but actual fabric choices were made as I went along.

For the construction on SPELLBOUND, I used purchased 9" tear-away foundations. On other quilts I've used foundations that are a combination of Log Cabin and Pineapple variations on one

Log Cabin

sheet. It's very expedient and convenient to use these. If you want to save money, create a different size, or make a customized block, typing or graph paper will work fine. You can either draw the sewing lines on each block or use a copy machine for larger quilts.

I used the piecing method as described by Dixie Haywood and Jane Hall in the book *Perfect Pineapples*. For SPELLBOUND, the fabric was placed on top of the foundation sheet. This placement feels normal. I've also tried placing the fabric under the foundation and sewn directly on the paper. This method feels very awkward at first but is more accurate than the first method. After completion of a block or two, both methods will seem easy.

SPELLBOUND
Pineapple Log Cabin
foundation piecing
pattern
shown at 75%

Allison Lockwood

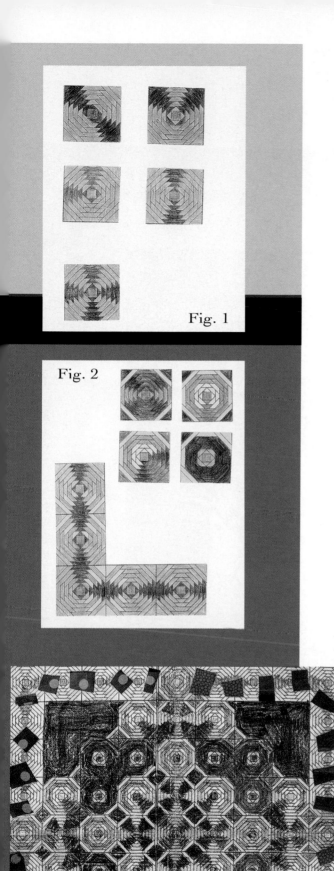

Fig. 1

Fig. 2

Fig. 3

There are a few pointers that will help you sew Log Cabin blocks on paper foundations:

• Use a pencil to write a description of each fabric (for example, dots, pink) on the area of the foundation paper in which it is to be placed. This prevents sewing fabric in the wrong place.

• Use a very short machine stitch. I set my stitch length between 1 and 2 on my machine. A small stitch will make the paper easier to remove when the quilt top is completed. Also, tearing the paper off will put some strain on the seam so it's important that a loose stitch is not used.

• Leave all the foundations on until your top is completed and you're ready to baste.

• Fill a spray bottle full of water. Spray the paper on back of the block really well before attempting to remove the paper. It will come off a lot easier.

• It took three weeks to remove the paper from my quilt. Be patient about the time it takes to remove the paper. A Pineapple Log Cabin not sewn on a foundation will probably end up in your UFO (unfinished objects) pile!

• If your strips aren't sewn exactly on the sewing line of the foundation, don't worry about it. There is one exception, though. Make sure you are sewing perfectly on the line where the seams come to the outer edge of the block. If you're off here, when you sew your blocks together the seams won't match.

DESIGNING THE BLOCK

What makes the Pineapple Log Cabin block so fascinating is the infinite ways you can change the appearance of the block by manipulating colors.

I've colored in blocks to demonstrate the possibilities. First, I've colored the blocks the way most people think of as a Pineapple (Fig. 1). Then I've colored in blocks as used in SPELLBOUND (Fig. 2). Last, I've made some new colorations (Fig. 3). Any of these blocks can be repeated in a quilt or can be used in combinations to make a complex-looking puzzle.

Other ideas include mixing Pineapple and non-pineapple Log Cabin blocks, using two different sized blocks, or placing all the blocks on point.

Allison Lockwood

BUTTERFLIES ARE FREE

77" x 88", Kimono fabrics, sashiko thread
Machine pieced, hand appliquéd & quilted

54

Lois Monieson

When visiting Japan in 1992, I purchased a book of Log Cabin designs by Kuroha Shizuko. I was flabbergasted! They were Log Cabin designs, but they didn't look the least bit like any I'd seen before.

Lois Monieson
Kingston, Ontario, Canada

MY QUILTMAKING

In 1985, I took a quilting course at a summer program and loved it. One of my first quilting teachers was Doris Waddell, who has been a winner twice in AQS shows. Another early teacher of mine was Patricia Morris, who inspired me to aspire to excellence.

An aunt of mine, who lived on a farm, was a quilter. I always told her I wanted to quilt but never got around to doing it while she was alive. I hope she knows how much I enjoy quilting now.

I love to go to big quilt shows and conferences and take as many workshops as I can. The continuing stimulation of attending these events and entering competitions where my quilts are shown makes me want to make more quilts. I also buy many quilt, art, and design books and quilt magazines.

I plan to keep attending workshops and conferences, entering competitions, and buying books for as long as I can. This cross-country stimulation and the many friends I make through participation replace the by-gone days of the quilting bee for me.

MY QUILT

I have always liked the Log Cabin design and had already made two Log Cabin quilts, but this quilt was inspired by Kuroha Shizuko's Clamshell design shown in her book. The quilt uses uneven logs that result in a 5½" finished block. In her quilt Kuroha Shizuko stacked them on top of each other, but I interlocked blocks as Moneca Calvert does in some of her Clamshell quilts.

This quilt is made from Japanese Yukata fabric I purchased during two trips to Japan and in Berkeley, California. The border and some of the other fabrics in the center were cut from used kimonos. The butterflies were cut from an antique kimono as well. I am pleased with the quilt but wish I could have had a few more fabric choices for some of the Clamshells.

Since making BUTTERFLIES ARE FREE, I have made another uneven Log Cabin design. In these quilts, I have stretched the Log Cabin design to encompass a culture other than my own by using Japanese fabrics and elements of Japanese design. I am pleased that this quilt tells my story.

BUTTERFLIES ARE FREE

When I start to design a quilt, I usually begin with the fabric. I search through books and magazines for ideas and to make sure I don't copy directly from anyone else.

I don't use a computer, but I do use copies of blocks to make cut-and-paste mock-ups of different possibilities. For BUTTERFLIES ARE FREE, I used a 5½" block. I finished the blocks for the borders first and put them on my design wall. The center clamshells are cut from 49 different fabrics. I used 22 of these same fabrics for the half clamshells.

Four uneven Log Cabin (Fig. 1) blocks were required to make each clamshell (full-sized pattern on page 57). Besides the clamshell color, four other colors from interlocking clamshells had to be decided on before I could piece even one block.

Log Cabin

To plan my interlocking color arrangement, I cut out a clamshell from cheesecloth and pinned all the precut logs needed for one clamshell to the cheesecloth. These pinned together clamshells were arranged and re-arranged on my design wall until I decided on a pleasing arrangement (Fig. 2). The logs were unpinned from each cheesecloth clamshell and sewn together.

When I quilt, I use a 12" hoop. I basted the layers together using a 2" to 3" grid. I do not premark quilt tops before basting. To mark BUTTERFLIES ARE FREE, I cut templates from heavy plastic template material. I traced each segment on clear self-adhesive shelf plastic. The clamshell rings were cut out and placed on the quilt, following a diagram. Some pinning is required, and new rings are needed from time to time.

Each appliquéd butterfly is a little quilt. I used the method Ann Boyce calls "three-dimensional appliqué." Each butterfly includes a top layer, cotton batting, and a backing. I quilted each butterfly by hand with sashiko thread and satin stitched around the edges of each block, cutting away the fabric close to the satin stitching. Placing tear-away stabilizer behind each butterfly, I satin stitched around the cut edge.

Each butterfly was attached to the top of the quilt just underneath the slightly rippled edge to give the appearance that it is just lightly resting on the quilt.

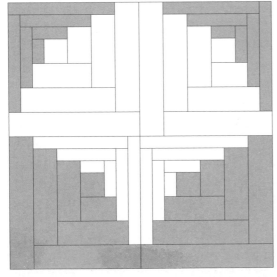

Fig. 1

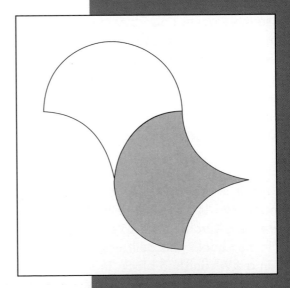

Fig. 2

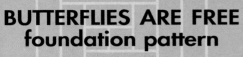

BUTTERFLIES ARE FREE
foundation pattern
shown at 100%

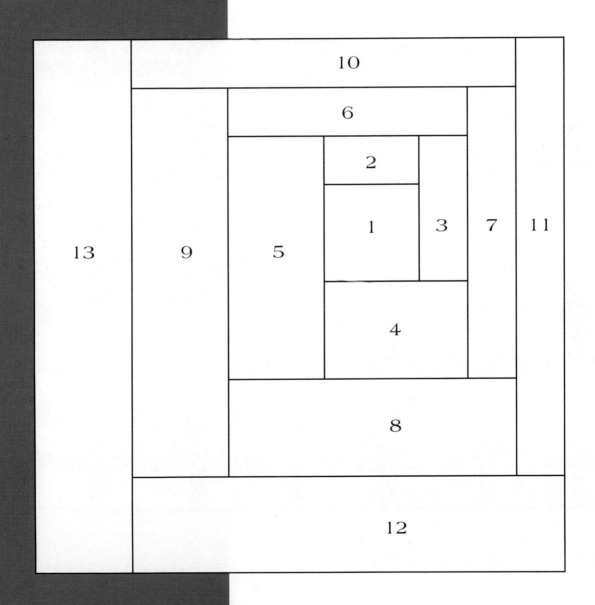

HOMAGE TO MONDRIAAN VII: A GREEN QUILT

64" x 64", Cottons, cotton & monofilament threads
Machine pieced & quilted

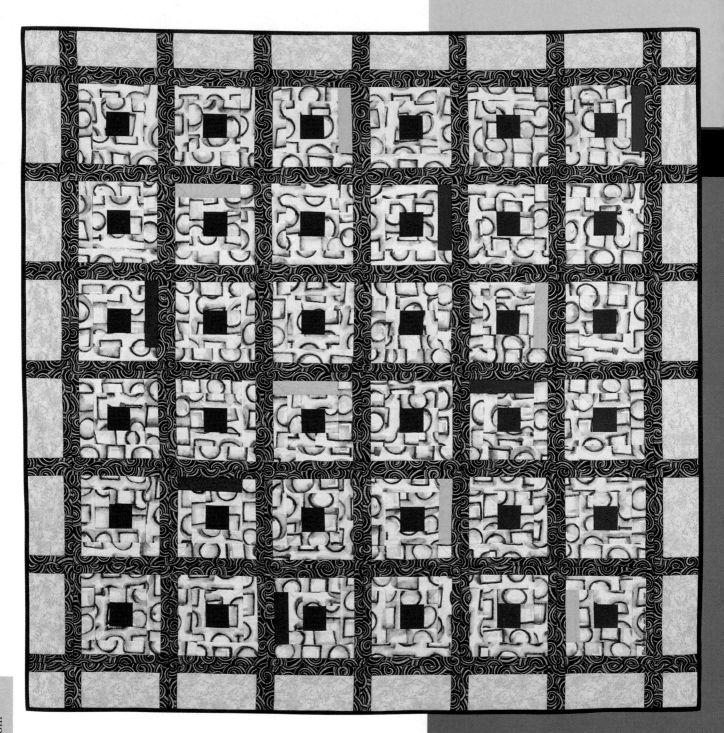

Meiny Vermaas-van der Heide

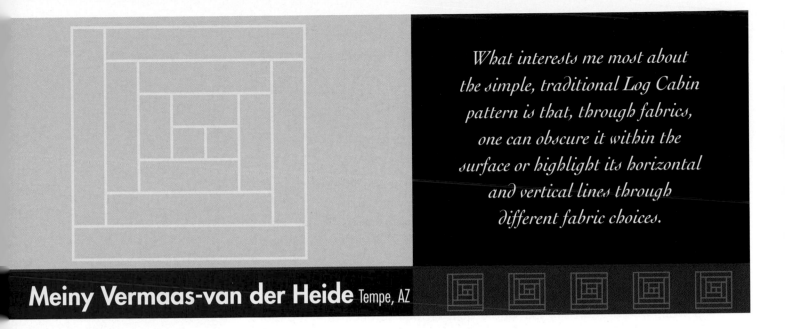

What interests me most about the simple, traditional Log Cabin pattern is that, through fabrics, one can obscure it within the surface or highlight its horizontal and vertical lines through different fabric choices.

Meiny Vermaas-van der Heide Tempe, AZ

MY QUILTMAKING

I clearly remember the picture in *Ariadne*, the Dutch needle arts magazine that introduced me to quilts – it was an attic bedroom with a Log Cabin quilt in pinks and grays on the bed. So much did I desire to have such a beautiful quilt for my own bed, that I decided to make my first quilt in 1982, the only quilt I ever made in the Netherlands. Although it was pieced and quilted on the sewing machine, it was still three years in the making, mostly because of the lack of suitable filler material and a floor space big enough to stretch the layers.

Upon moving to the USA in 1985, I wanted to learn more about quilts firsthand. Little did I know how quilts could ease foreigners like me into the American social fabric. Here I found quilts to be very interwoven with the country's historical and cultural heritage. I felt kinship with the women immigrants, the westward trekking pioneers who had come before me. Before women had the right to vote, many a quilt was made as a way to speak out. As a foreigner here, I do not have the right to vote, but I can use my talents to voice my concerns through my quilts.

MY QUILT

This quilt was inspired by Mondriaan paintings from his Pier and Ocean series and by an exhibit of Vincent van Gogh drawings I saw in a Dutch museum in 1990. I suddenly realized why Nancy Crow had had us work in black and white solids, black and white prints, neutral and natural colors, and, as a grand finale, in full color in her Positive/Negative quilt design workshop.

Especially fascinating to me in the exhibit were the "scribbled" drawings, where the density of the scribbled pencil marks caused value differences and beautiful visual texture at the same time. I could envision what I might do with black and white "scribble" fabric I had bought earlier. In the midst of my "Homage to Mondriaan" series, I began to incorporate the scribbled fabrics.

My quilts are my voice. Many of my quilts are labeled as "green quilts," which stands for environmental concern expressed in a positive, open-ended way. The charge in the Bible's book of Genesis for us to be "stewards of the earth" is my inspiration for making "green quilts."

ACHIEVING AN HEIRLOOM LOOK

Having made many Log Cabin-based quilts, I offer these tips and techniques for creating flat quilt surfaces with an heirloom-style look.

PIECING LOG CABIN BLOCKS

• Try not to push or pull the fabric strips. Be patient and let the feed dogs do the work.
• When using a bright center square with lighter strips, zigzag the seam allowances before cutting the bright strip into squares, so fraying of the colored center will not show through the lighter fabric in the finished Log Cabin blocks.
• When pressing Log Cabin blocks, press all seam allowances away from the center square

and let the fabric cool down before adding the next strip or log. Fabric will stretch when slightly wet and hot from the steam. Also, keep in mind that pressing means holding the iron in place for 10 seconds, then lifting the iron to move to the next part to be pressed. Sliding a hot steaming iron over the surface will stretch the fabrics excessively.

PIN-BASTING THE QUILT SANDWICH

The way that I pin baste my quilt sandwich seems to have a great deal to do with achieving an heirloom look in my quilts. In a 1987 workshop, Harriet Hargrave introduced me to using a batting containing cotton to create machine-quilted quilts with an old-fashioned look and touch.

Using batting containing cotton and cotton fabrics, I am able to stretch the layers of the quilt sandwich and "glue" them vertically on a wall, where I can see the whole quilt surface at once and straighten the layers more easily. The vertical lines of paneling in the hallway where I pin baste become guidelines for squaring up the horizontal and vertical lines of the quilt sandwich.

Use the following methods to pin baste:
• Stretch the quilt backing (wrong side facing toward you) using 2" masking tape. Put the masking tape around the edges, as if you were stretching it in a frame. First, put pieces of masking tape at the top edge and each corner. Put more masking tape along the top edge, because it will carry the most weight. During this process, it is possible that you may need to re-tape certain parts to get the back tautly stretched. Depending on the size of the quilt, the quality of the masking tape, and the humidity in the air, the quilt sandwich will stay up anywhere from three hours to three days.
• "Glue" the batting on top of the quilt backing by gently stroking the batting, and fasten with large quilter's pins at the top and sides.
• "Glue" the quilt top over the batting by gently stroking from left to right and top to bottom, following the direction of the seam allowances. Fasten with large quilter's pins around the edges of the quilt top, moving the quilter's pins from the batting to the quilt top and adding more as needed. During this process, keep the horizontal seam lines horizontal and the vertical seam lines vertical. Re-position the quilter's pins if necessary.
• The quilt sandwich is now ready for pin basting with 1" safety pins. I usually place pins 3" to 5" apart, but the spacing you use will depend on the type of batting and how you plan to machine quilt the sandwich. In HOMAGE TO MONDRIAAN VII, I put five safety pins in each block: one in the center square and in each corner of the second round. I prefer to spend more time pinning than having to rip out machine quilting because of "false pleats."
• Pin baste from left to right (when right-handed), putting a horizontal row of safety pins in the middle of the quilt first. Alternate, adding a horizontal row of safety pins above and below this middle row.

Log Cabin

Meiny Vermaas-van der Heide

• For pin basting the top rows, you might want to use a small step ladder, and sitting down on a stool makes pin basting the bottom rows a lot easier.

It is very important that the safety pins go through all layers of the quilt sandwich. To pin baste:
• Insert safety pin through all layers.
• Feel how the point of the safety pin touches the wall.
• Lift the quilt sandwich just slightly with the safety pin in your right hand and at the same time keep the quilt sandwich down with the pointing and middle fingers of your left hand.
• Bring the point of the safety pin up again.
• Close the safety pin using both hands, your right hand to bring the visible bottom part of the safety pin toward the other part stuck through the quilt sandwich, and your left pointing finger or middle finger to keep the point of the safety pin up. Older brass safety pins work the best because they are more flexible.

After you have closed the safety pin, you should not be able to move it, and on the back of the quilt ¼" of each safety pin should be visible. The drawback of using safety pins is that they can leave small holes in the quilt top, but these disappear when the quilt is laundered, the final step in creating an heirloom look. If a safety pin cuts a thread in one of the fabrics in the quilt top, the tiny hole can be stabilized with fray sealant.

When the entire center is pin basted, take the quilt down and replace the quilter's pins around the edges with safety pins. I find it easier to do this on a horizontal surface, so the safety pins can all be put in facing the same direction. That way they can be removed more easily while you are stabilizing the outside edges with machine quilting.

COMPLETING THE HEIRLOOM EFFECT

• Upon finishing a quilt, I put it through the gentle cycle in the washing machine using cold water and Orvus® paste or Synthrapol®. Afterward, the quilt is blocked (gently flattened and straightened by patting it by hand) on a cotton sheet on the carpet in my studio, where it air dries in one or two days, depending on the humidity in the air. The quilt sandwich will shrink 1" to 2" in comparison to the quilt top, depending on the type of batting that was used.
• Synthrapol® is the detergent of choice if there still are problems with colors bleeding despite washing all fabrics before using them.
• Do not panic when you see the backing showing through in the wet quilt or when you see needle holes from your stitching in the wet quilt. Both will disappear when the quilt has dried. So will the small holes from the safety pins.
• As soon as my quilts are dry, they go directly from the floor to the design wall, for documentation in slides and pictures, before they are ever folded for storage or shipping.

LOG CABIN
patterns
¼" seam allowance included.

Included in this section are four different sizes of full templates for the traditional Log Cabin pattern. Select the size most appropriate for your fabrics and project plans and try your own hand at this popular pattern.

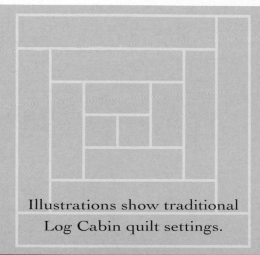

Illustrations show traditional Log Cabin quilt settings.

Barn Raising

Sunshine and Shadow

Straight Furrow

Zigzag

LOG CABIN
patterns
¼" seam allowance included.

6" BLOCK

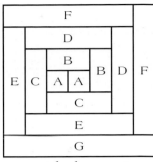

patch placement

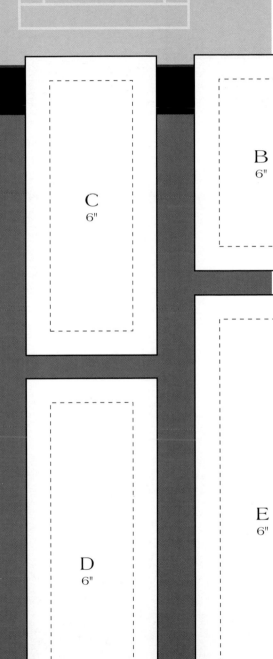

C
6"

B
6"

A
6"

D
6"

E
6"

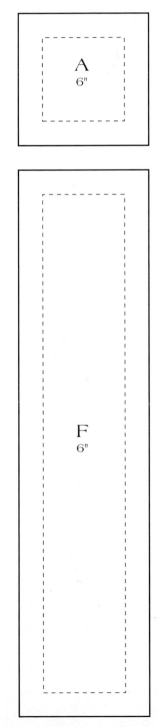

F
6"

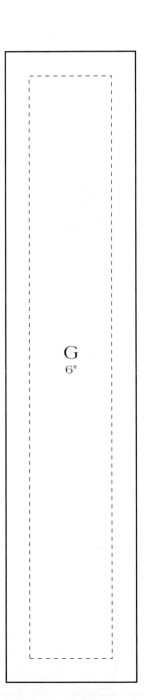

G
6"

8" BLOCK

C
8"

B
8"

A
8"

D
8"

E
8"

F
8"

G
8"

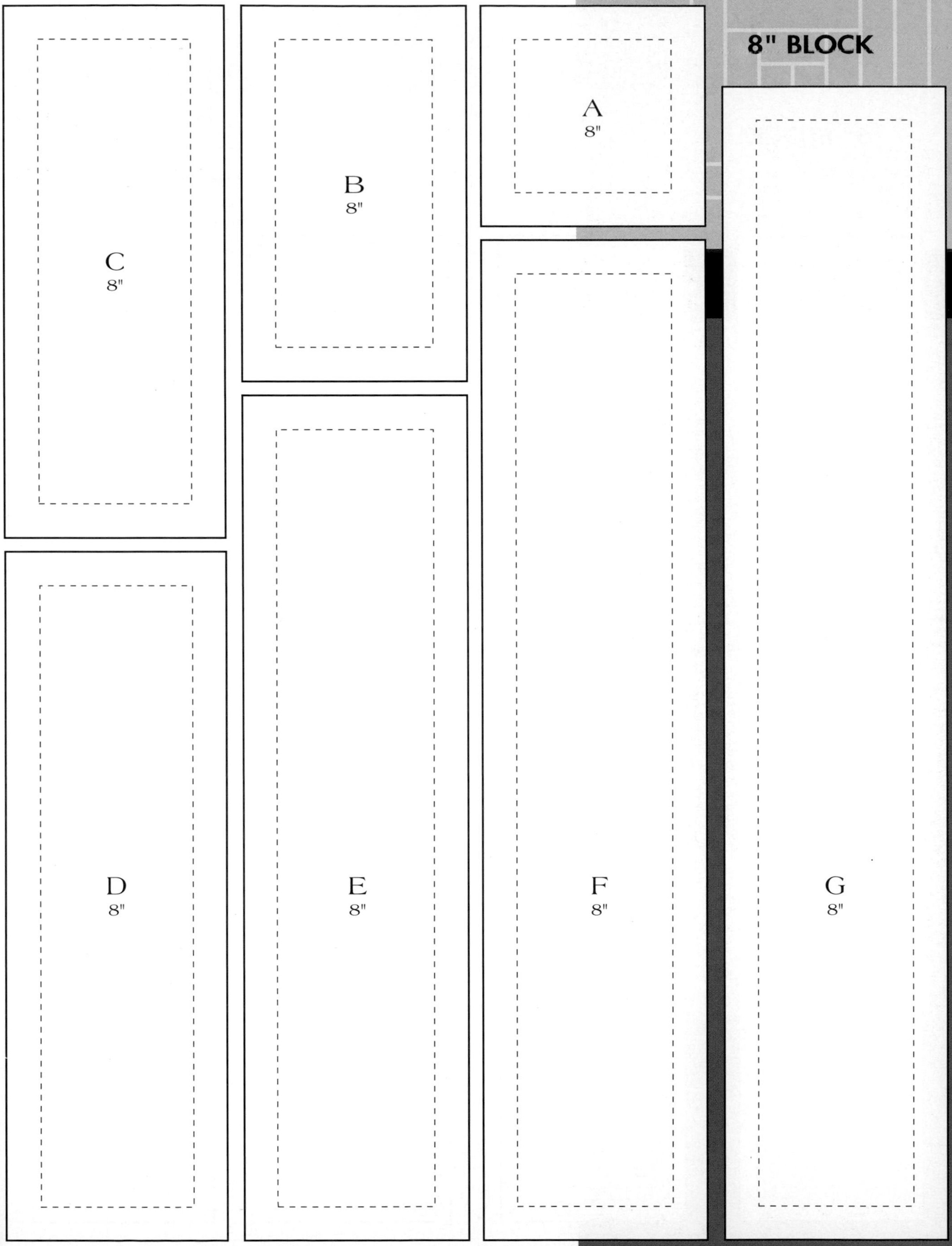

LOG CABIN
patterns
¼" seam allowance included.

10" BLOCK

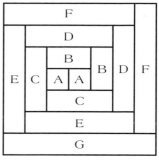

patch placement

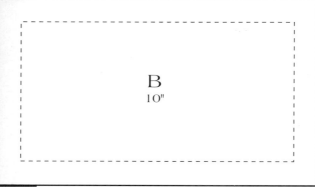

A
10"

B
10"

C
10"

D
10"

E
10"

F
10"

place on fold

G
10"

LOG CABIN
patterns
¼" seam allowance included.

12" BLOCK

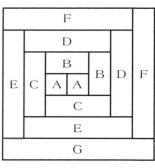

patch placement

A
12"

B
12"

C
12"

D
12"

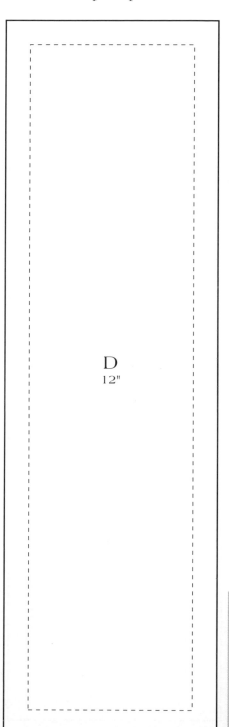

E
12"

place on fold

F
12"

place on fold

G
12"

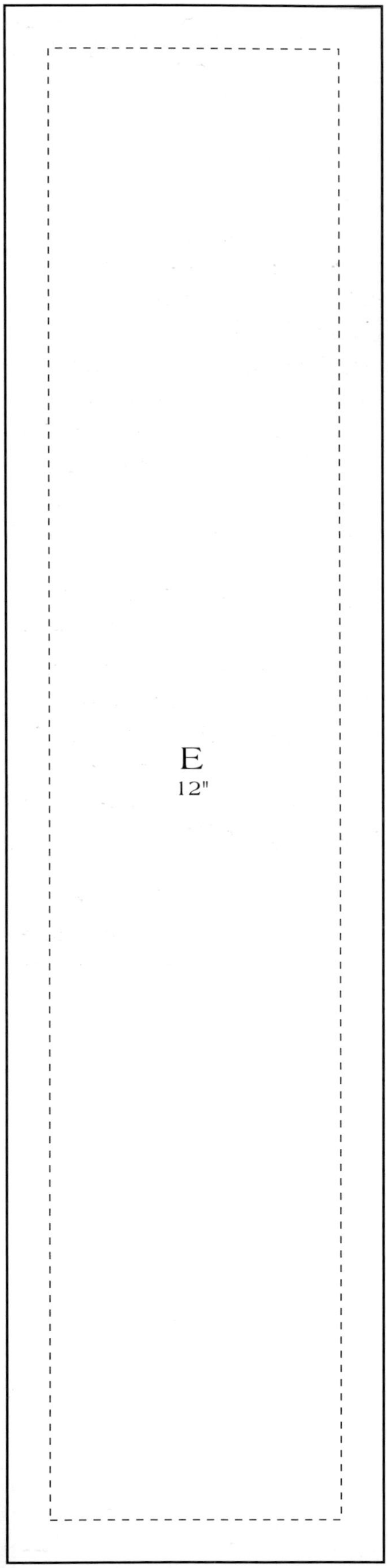

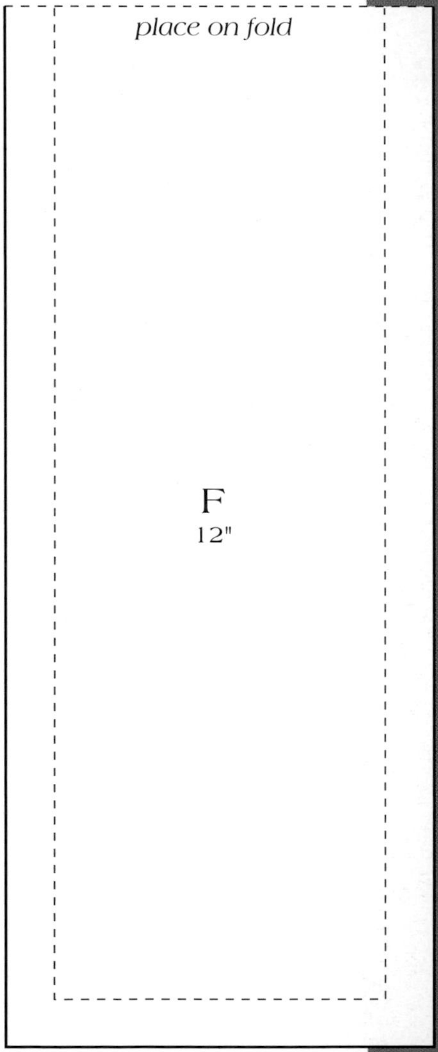

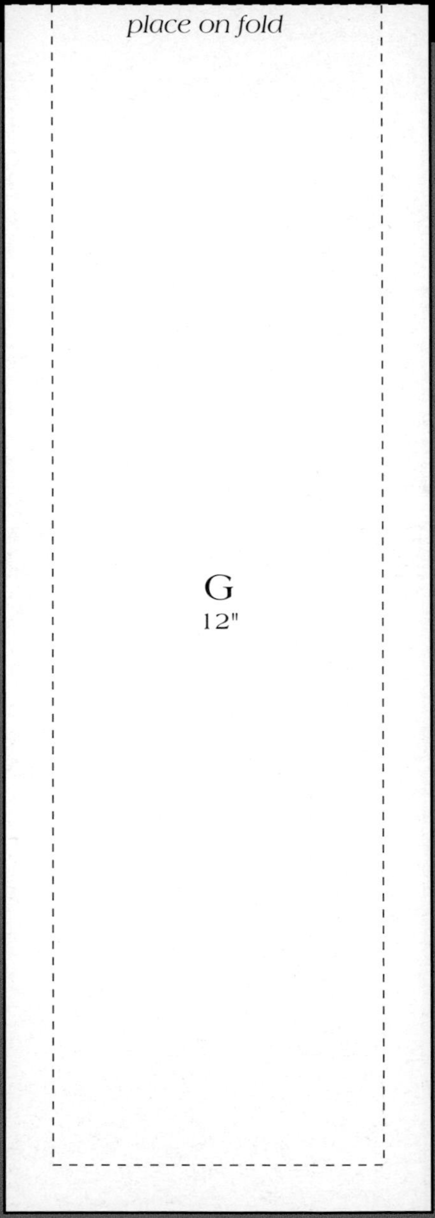

OHIO STAR QUILTS

The Ohio Star block is known by many names, depending on the color and value placement in its patches. Mosaic, Texas Star, Eastern Star, Variable Star, and Star of Hope are just a few of the titles that have been handed down over the years. Only two patch shapes are needed for this easy-to-assemble block, a square and a quarter-square triangle. But wait until you see what the contestants have done with it. The block has been divided, subdivided, outlined, and stretched. Our foremothers would have been surprised and delighted.

In this section of *Editor's Choice*, you will find descriptions of some interesting and unusual techniques. Corinne Appleton will show you how to emphasize the stars' lines by appliquéing narrow strips around the seams of an off-center block. The traditional embellishment called couching can be easily adapted to the sewing machine, as described on page 85. Learn how to create a complex border to fit your Ohio Star blocks (page 71).

Turn to pages 90 to 95 for Ohio Star block patterns in sizes ranging from 3" to 14". Use these patterns to create a traditional or contemporary Ohio Star quilt of your own design.

STAR FIELD

66" x 77", Cotton
Machine pieced & hand quilted

Maggie Potter

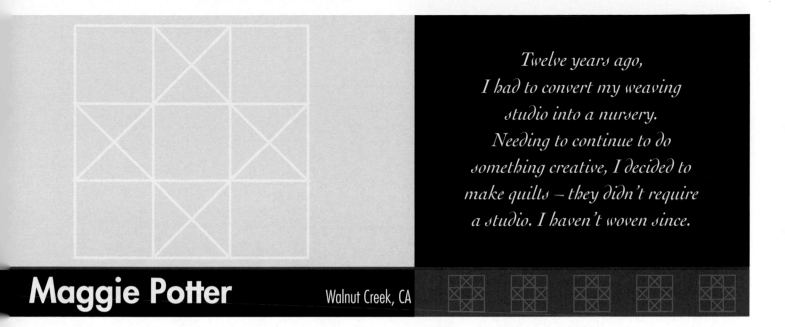

*Twelve years ago,
I had to convert my weaving
studio into a nursery.
Needing to continue to do
something creative, I decided to
make quilts — they didn't require
a studio. I haven't woven since.*

Maggie Potter
Walnut Creek, CA

MY QUILTMAKING

It was in 1983, the year my first daughter was born, that I began quilting. Before that, I had been a weaver and had also been very involved with surfing. With my three daughters, I find I drive across town at least six times a day. But, being an artist, I will always find time to create because that is part of my life.

I have two close friends who know my work well, having seen it develop over the years. They cheer me on when I become tired and discouraged, and my husband Frank, is also very supportive. Years ago, I had the opportunity to see the Esprit quilt collection in San Francisco, which was most inspiring.

STAR FIELD is my fifth quilt with an elaborate border — borders can be very tedious. I don't have a specific quilt in mind for my next project, but it probably won't have a border!

MY QUILT

This quilt was made specially for the MAQS contest and was an exciting project. I have used the Ohio Star pattern only once before, but I enjoy making quilts with different star patterns, my favorite being the Evening Star, a Four-Patch design.

STAR FIELD consists of 99 Ohio Star blocks, each 4½", plus multiple borders. The back is also pieced. I always add extra unrelated squares to the back. The entire quilt has over 4,500 pieces, all tea-dyed. I like the subtle color combinations and the sashing fabric, and I didn't want the sashing to stand out. I've found that the sashing can make or break a quilt.

I am very influenced by antique quilts. They have a great deal of character, and I enjoy the fact that they are not perfect. I don't worry about the points of stars being perfect or squares being exact. I am more concerned about the overall design. Antique quilts, with their imperfections, are wonderful.

ADDING BORDERS TO QUILTS

Many of the quilts I make have intricate borders. The many different patterned fabrics in my blocks generate a lot of movement. Borders are frequently needed to enclose this movement and prevent the eye from meandering off the quilt.

The border is added merely to enhance the overall design. I piece the center blocks first, often repeating no fabric combination more than once. When this is completed, I add one border at a time. If the quilt is elaborate in composition, I will use only one to two fabrics in the border. In STAR FIELD, the border colors were kept to a minimum. However, in the widest segment of the border, I used numerous colored fabrics so the border would not become too repetitious.

I used ½" strips of fabric in between the borders to ease the fabric into laying completely flat. I do not try to match the corners or make the borders connect perfectly. It's my belief a quilt should appear somewhat unplanned.

OHIO LANDSCAPE

*78" x 63", Cotton fabrics, commercial &
hand dyed, hand printed, hand marbled
Machine pieced & quilted*

Ohio Star

Gertrude Embree & Gayle Wallace

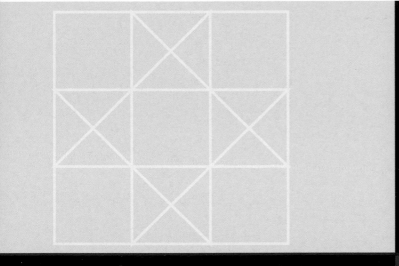

Gertrude Embree & Gayle Wallace Shreveport, LA

I first discovered the Ohio Star pattern in a piece of handwoven Swedish folk art and adapted it to my own weaving. When I moved on to quiltmaking, the star moved on with me.

Commentary by Gertrude Embree

MY QUILTMAKING

Gayle and I enjoy working together and look forward to collaborating again. I began quiltmaking in the early 1960s and made several bed quilts for my family in the 1970s, but it wasn't until the late 1980s that I found my loom shoved in a corner while my fabric collection grew. Designing is always a struggle for me, and self doubt is a gremlin I constantly fight. But I love to create, in quilting and as a closet cartoonist.

I choose to make quilts because I love their special surface texture and potential for creativity on a large scale. I also enjoy the community of creative people in the quilt world and their willingness to share their discoveries.

Gayle started quilting in 1985 and has since taught over 1,500 students, a number of whom have gone on to win awards. Gayle makes quilts to please herself. Seeing someone softly touch and appreciate the work that went into the making of a quilt is a great joy for her. It was Gayle who encouraged me to enter this quilt in the MAQS contest.

MY QUILT

It was great fun to play with the Ohio Star, an old pattern I had worked with often in my weaving. I began the design on my computer, using draw and paint software. Several quilts emerged from this computer play; however, a painting by Japanese artist Toshinobu Onosato inspired me to begin again. Using graph paper, I worked out the design. At the same time the quilt design was evolving, I was also having a lot of fun experimenting with fabric painting and printing.

The colors in the quilt represent the blues and greens of our beautiful Earth which is the central sphere. Ohio itself is, of course, the large star within the sphere – blue for its great river. The woods and fields of my childhood home in southern Ohio are nestled in the center. A scrap of my mother's dress is at the very heart. Farmlands surround the circle, and corn stars symbolize the cities. Like many of my quilts, this is a "green quilt," which carries a message of hope for the health of our planet. The machine quilting was done by Gayle, using a monofilament thread.

DESIGNING

To plan my quilt, I developed a full working plan. I drew it on graph paper, letting each square of the grid equal ½", so it took four of the grid squares to equal one inch.

If you compare the graph-paper drawing to the quilt, you will see I did not follow the drawing faithfully in all details. The placement of the main shapes is the same, but I improvised the centers of the corner stars. There are a number of other ideas in the drawing that are not in the quilt...I changed my mind!

The pencil lines, especially visible on the lower right side, were my doodles for proposed quilting lines. Gayle used a different design.

Ohio Star

In a drawing like this, the color placement is only approximate. This design becomes a general guide rather than a precise plan that must be followed in every detail.

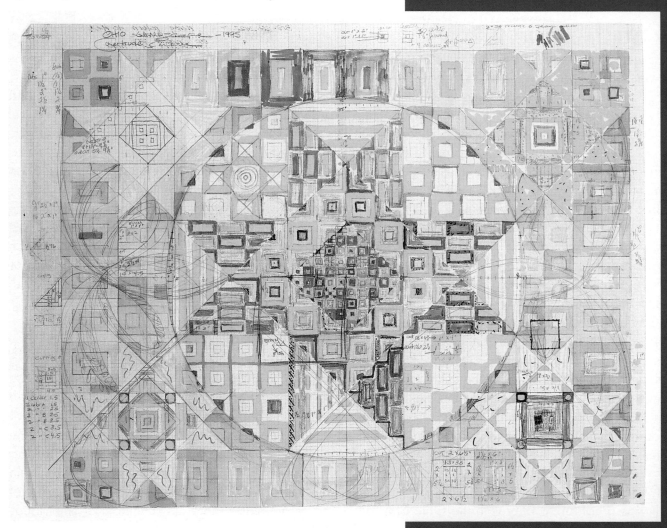

Gertrude Embree & Gayle Wallace

CRYSTAL STAR

88" x 88", Cotton & acetate/rayon
Machine pieced, hand embroidered & machine quilted

Izumi Takamori

I hope looking at my quilt gives people ideas about how they could develop their own designs for quilts.

MY QUILTMAKING

For years, I experimented with knitting, embroidery, sewing, and making a wide variety of other needle arts. Then 17 years ago, I saw my first art quilt, and I began to take quilting classes to learn proper techniques. I studied for two years. Creating quilts satisfies my urges to touch, collect, and experiment with many different kinds of fabric.

Last year, I signed up for a class from Emiko Toda Loeb when she was teaching in Japan. She gave me an assignment to make an Eight-Pointed Star quilt. I have always loved star designs, and was inspired by the Ohio Star pattern, which many people love. I was able to complete CRYSTAL STAR before the end of the class, but it was only this year that I had time to add the embroidery.

I now have a quilt shop and work every day in the shop, which keeps me very busy, but I plan to continue to make quilts for my own satisfaction and also for entering into competitive quilt shows.

MY QUILT

When I began CRYSTAL STAR, I knew I wanted to make a white quilt with many kinds of white fabric, lace, and embroidery. Cotton, acetate-rayon, and cotton lace are all included in the top, which was constructed by using fast machine-piecing techniques. The quilt was then machine quilted with metallic thread. Hand embroidery was added with cotton, polyester, and rayon threads, knitting yarn, and sashiko thread. I worked with the Ohio Star pattern again, as back art planned for CRYS-

TAL STAR, but this Ohio Star design instead ended up on the front of a quilt I call PUZZLED STAR. Both of these Ohio Star quilts were fun to make and exiting to finish. I like both of them and would like the challenge of creating another design using the Ohio Star pattern.

DESIGNING

In Emiko Toda Loeb's workshops I developed the design for CRYSTAL STAR (drawing on page 77). As you'll note from comparing it with the photo of the finished quilt on page 75, I made a few changes when I actually made the quilt. Variations in the amount of contrast between star and background fabrics also make some stars and star parts much more visible than others in the final quilt.

Right: Close-up of CRYSTAL STAR
Below: Layout for CRYSTAL STAR

ALL CATS GO TO HEAVEN

60" x 60", Cotton fabric & batting, various threads, buttons
Machine appliquéd, broderie perse, hand beaded, machine pieced

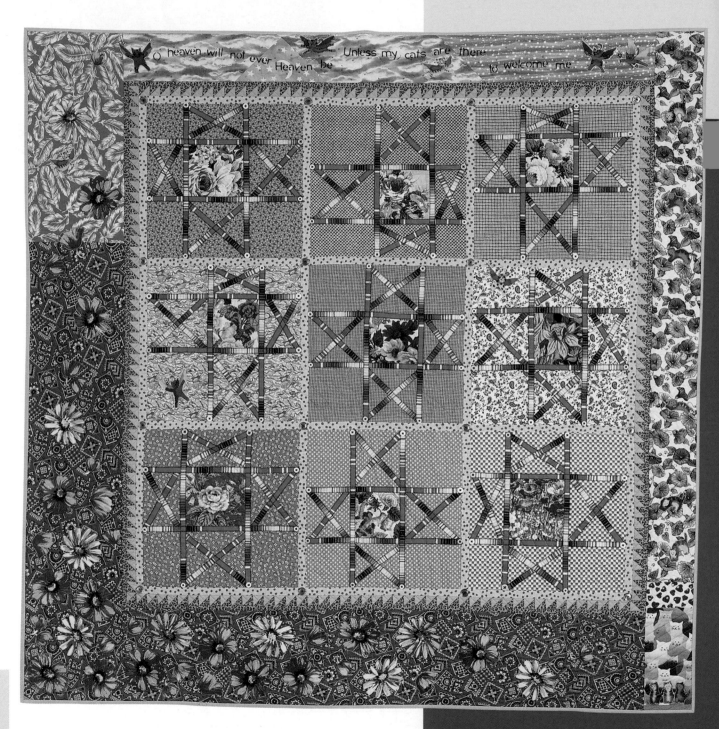

Corinne Appleton

EDITOR'S CHOICE New Quilts from an Old Favorite

ALL CATS GO TO HEAVEN seemed to help make itself, right down to the wonderful flying "angel" cat fabric that appeared in one of my favorite quilt shops the day before I needed it.

MY QUILTMAKING

The impending birth of my first niece in 1987 found me working on something that resembled a quilt, and when my enthusiasm overflowed, I also made a Log Cabin throw. These two pseudo-quilts would have been my entire quilting legacy were it not for the unwavering support of my father.

People often seem to think my quilts spring to life easily and magically. They don't. There is often near agony involved in my quiltmaking, whether it is related to the message, the design, or the construction. ALL CATS GO TO HEAVEN was somewhat an exception, but I credit this to the fact that I had already spent a considerable amount of time exploring alternatives on computer quilt design programs.

Often, women refer to their quilting as a hobby, sometimes as a passion, and only rarely as an obsession. I live, breathe, and dream quilts. I make quilts because I must. They are my voice.

MY QUILT

I viewed the wonderful Log Cabin quilts in the 1995 MAQS contest and found myself intrigued with making an Ohio Star quilt for the 1996 contest. A new user of computer design software, I began to experiment. My original design has yet to be made, but with a stack of new fabrics, I began rotary slicing, and a different Ohio Star quilt emerged.

Comprised of nine stars that represent the nine lives that folklore has attributed to cats, this quilt celebrates the lives of five cats I had lost. These stars shine in the heavenly garden where I envision my five cats gamboling happily. Of course, they are not alone in their feline heaven. There are many who have gone before them and they, too, are there.

"O heaven will not ever Heaven be Unless my cats are here with me," an epitaph from a pet cemetery, perfectly expresses my feelings and, I suspect, those of many fortunate enough to have known love from those wonderful bundles of fur.

USING APPLIQUÉD STRIPS

ALL CATS GO TO HEAVEN began with the idea of distorting the basic Ohio Star block. Working with the computer program, I decided to keep the blocks themselves square, but to distort the star within the boundaries of the block. When the idea of emphasizing the blocks' lines by using appliquéd strips made its way into my consciousness, the concept of each block being slightly different from the others seemed appropriate.

There are many ways you could modify my quilt. Think of the defining strips as frames. The quilt block centers could feature family and friends' portraits. Even a small Ohio Star block could be drafted and fit within the confines of the larger star (Fig. 1 on the following page).

The finished size of the blocks in ALL CATS GO TO HEAVEN is 14½", but the directions given use a 15½" square to simplify the math.

Step 1

Cut one 15½" square from your background fabric. Starch the block to stabilize it. If you are using one or two background fabrics for the entire quilt, starch the fabrics as yardage, then cut your blocks from the fabrics.

The most important rule when spray starching your fabric is to give the starch plenty of time to be absorbed into the fibers before ironing. I often spray a group of fabrics, roll them up, then clean and oil my sewing machine before ironing.

If you are using yardage, you can then iron as usual. If you have pre-cut your blocks, it is important that you press, not iron, them. Running the iron back and forth will leave you moaning over a pile of blocks that once were square.

Step 2

To design your distorted block, choose the size and position you will use for the center of your Ohio Star. You have two options for the block center and will probably want to vary them both in your quilt.

First, your center can be cut to the traditional one-ninth of the surface area of the block. With a finished size of 15" x 15", this means a 5" x 5" square.

Alternatively, you can cut a square or rectangle in any measurement that is close to the traditional center square size, but slightly "off." Even very small changes in the size are effective. Try 4½" x 5½", or 5" x 6".

The effectiveness of your block center depends as much on its placement on the background as it does on its altered size. Place your block center in the approximate middle of your background square. If your center is a rectangle or a square smaller than 5", you may choose to make this the permanent position for the center.

NOTE: If you are using a 5" square, it is essential to the block design that you move your center so that it is not in the middle of the block (Fig. 2). Otherwise, you will end up with a traditional Ohio Star block rather than the distorted version we are making.

All of the blocks used in ALL CATS GO TO HEAVEN consist of centers that were first placed roughly in the middle of the background and then moved a small distance.

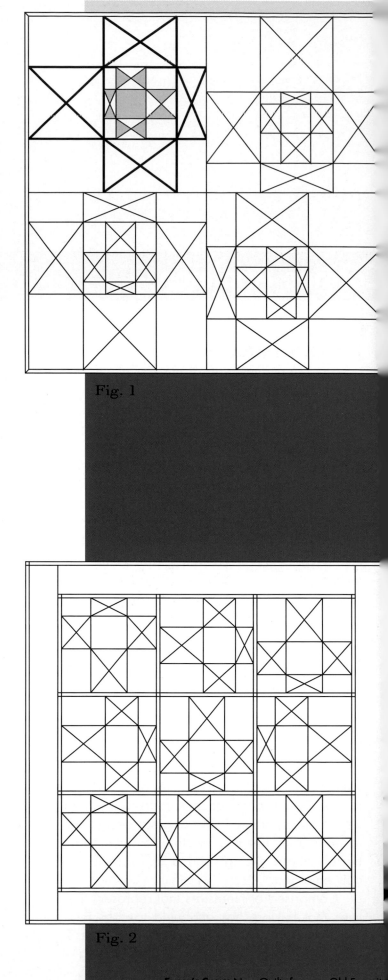

Fig. 1

Fig. 2

Ohio Star

80

Corinne Appleton

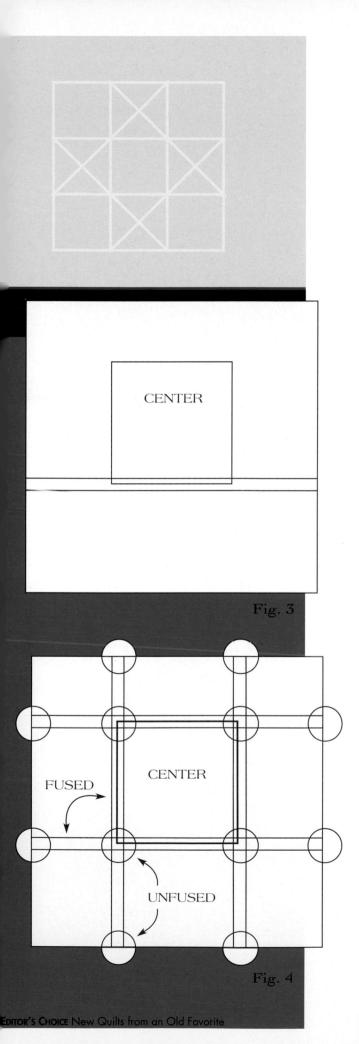

Fig. 3

Fig. 4

Step 3

Cut a 15½" x 2¼" piece of paper-backed fusible web. Fuse it to the back of the fabric you have chosen to define your star, preferably on the lengthwise grain. From this piece, cut four ½"-wide strips. It is easier to cut through both the paper-backed fusible web and the fabric at once. Take advantage of your extra ¼" of width and begin your first cut slightly to the inside of it and you will achieve a straighter edge. Peel the paper backing from your four 15½" x ½" strips.

Step 4

Using a ruler to ensure you are an even distance from the edge of your quilt block, place a ½" strip from Step 3 on one of the four edges of your center square or rectangle. The placement of this strip should overlap the center's edge by ¼" so that the fusible web covers both the center and the background fabric equally along the length of the center's edge (Fig. 3).

With your iron set to the appropriate temperature, fuse the strip to the block as follows: Use the iron tip to fuse the area between the outside edge of the block and the point where the strip meets the center square or rectangle. Leave approximately 1" unfused at the outside edge and at the area where the strip and center meet. Next, fuse the strip over the center square or rectangle, being careful to avoid that 1" area on both sides of the center. Finally repeat the fusing directions on the portion of your ½" strip that extends to the other side of the block.

These steps are repeated three times to form an irregular Nine-Patch, as shown in Fig. 4.

HINT: If at any point in the construction of your block you discover you have accidentally fused a portion of a defining strip you didn't want fused, don't worry. The simple remedy is to apply the iron to that area until the glue softens and the fabric can be lifted gently, using a pin or seam ripper to release the edge. Be careful not to distort the strip by tugging or pulling. With enough time and heat the adhesive will release.

One other word of caution: Do not let your freshly unglued appliqué piece touch itself.

Corinne Appleton

Prepare another 2¼"-wide piece of your strip fabric with fusible web. Try to get the maximum length possible from your yardage. Cut the piece into ½"-wide strips.

The next step in making your star is to fill in the "X" that creates the points. This is not a step that requires precise measuring, and there is no formula because this is where the diversity in your blocks shows up. It helps to begin by cutting one end of a ½" strip at an angle of about 45 loose degrees. Using a pin, wiggle that cut end under the intersection of one of the corners of your center. With a pin or a finger holding that end in place but allowing it to pivot, follow an imaginary diagonal line to create a star point. The star tip should be embellished with a button or other object so that the tip appears defined and not blunted. The second option is to lay the diagonal strip on top of the straight strip and carefully cut the diagonal strip on an angle to match the edge of the straight strip. This option creates a sharper point that requires no embellishment.

Choose the style of point you want and prepare your fabric strip, always remembering this golden rule: The diagonal strips always end ¼" from the block edge to allow for a seam allowance (Fig. 5). If you think you will have any difficulty remembering this rule, mark your block ¼" in on every straight ½" strip after they are in place. Just remember to use a marking method that will not become permanent with the application of a hot iron.

Once your diagonal strips are in place, the iron is laid over the previously unfused straight strip's outside edge and the length of the diagonal to where it just touches the center. Only when all of the strips have been fused as described should the iron be applied to the center intersections where it will fuse two diagonal ends beneath two intersecting straight strips at the same time.

STEP 5

Your block is now ready for appliqué. Put a new size 70 heavy duty needle in your cleaned and oiled machine and thread it with your choice of contrasting or matching thread.

With a piece of stabilizer (typing-weight paper) beneath your block, the next step is the stitching. The appliqué can be done with any number of decorative stitches or a simple zigzag. In ALL CATS GO TO HEAVEN, a black blanket stitch contrasts with the multicolored stripe of its defining strips. BEYOND ECCENTRIC AND PUSHING CRAZY (page 83) was appliquéd with a very narrow and short zigzag done in black so as to blend into the defining strips and not distract from the planned chaos of the stars.

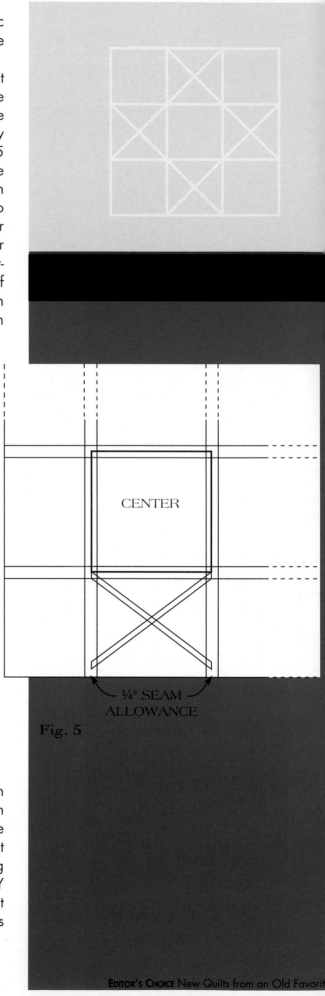

CENTER

¼" SEAM ALLOWANCE

Fig. 5

The most important technical contribution you can make to the success of your quilt block is to ensure that the line of appliqué is as straight as the edge of the ½" strips that outline your star.

Stitch the long straight strips first, making sure to backstitch at the end of each strip. The diagonal strips can be backstitched at their ends by machine if your thread and fabric are both dark and a perfect match. In most cases, you will find the appearance far preferable if you tug the upper thread to the reverse side, tie a square knot, and thread the ends through a row of stitches.

Once all the stitching is complete, turn the block over and remove your stabilizer. Carefully cut away the background fabric from beneath the center square or rectangle. Give your block a pressing, stick it up on your design wall, admire it, and then get busy making another one!

This block was intended to be one of the nine in ALL CATS GO TO HEAVEN; instead, it became an orphan after teaching me a lesson. The contrast between the crooked checks and the rigidly straight defining strips made the quilt top scream "TILT." If you use checks or plaids with this block pattern, be sure that they are printed or woven straight. Also, make sure that your defining strips are laid exactly parallel to the straight lines of the fabric's pattern.

BEYOND ECCENTRIC AND PUSHING CRAZY
47" x 47", 1996.

A LONG WAY FROM CINCINNATI

52" x 52", Cotton fabrics, rayon braids, cotton & rayon threads
Machine piecing, appliqué, and quilting (free motion) & couching

Ohio Star

Elizabeth Hendricks

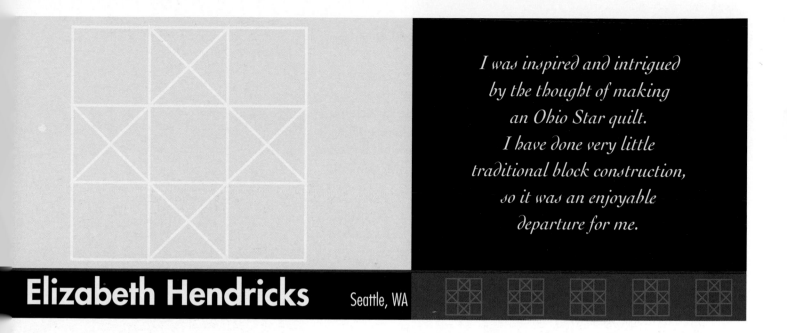

I was inspired and intrigued by the thought of making an Ohio Star quilt. I have done very little traditional block construction, so it was an enjoyable departure for me.

MY QUILTMAKING

I began quilting four-and-a-half years ago, with the birth of my nephew Joshua. In my former life, I was in product development and marketing. For almost 20 years my career was so consuming that I had little time for artistic pursuits.

I began quilting at home, which for me is a house barge on Seattle's Lake Union. I had a crazy way of working in the confines of the aft cabin and varied my methods depending upon how much the water might be moving.

After quilting during the storms of February 1993, I decided to get a little studio on land, a place where the walls stayed still and the floors didn't dance. I now have a little studio which is just a walk up the lake and across a drawbridge.

As a hobby I also fly small planes, so the designs or quilting lines in many of my pieces have a sense of floating. What I am working toward in quilting is for my command of technique to catch up with my imagination, to then see what emerges.

MY QUILT

I had not worked with the Ohio Star pattern before and was intrigued by its possibilities. I used to do business in Ohio and also now associate Ohio with quilt national and Nancy Crow's symposium, so the state has very positive associations.

I broke the Ohio Star design into two grids — the lower composed of horizontal and vertical lines, and the upper one of diagonals. I then pieced the lower Nine-Patch grid in cold colors,

and the upper in hot. When putting them back together, however, I couldn't see one grid for the other since the fabrics were opaque. I decided to cut curls through the layer of diagonals, so that once they were overlaid, the eye would connect the lines of the star. After quilting, I couched rayon braid to highlight the base structure of the stars.

I hope people enjoy tracing the straight-edged star within the colors of the curvilinear shapes and the secondary pattern (emphasized by the yellow wiggly shapes). I meant this piece to be up-beat and happy and hope that optimism is conveyed.

COUCHING TECHNIQUES

Couching is a type of embellishment traditionally used by hand embroiderers. Careful spiralling stitches are used to lay thick threads or decorative braids on the surface, often creating lovely curving designs.

Today, couching lends itself beautifully to contemporary quiltmaking. By adapting this method to the machine, one can easily embellish with decorative threads, braids, yarns, or ribbons. These can be used to outline appliquéd shapes, cover raw edges, enhance major design elements, or create an element of line. The possibilities and variations are endless.

In A LONG WAY FROM CINCINNATI machine couching is used in two ways. One is to enhance shape by outlining some of the appliqués. The other is to emphasize a line element in the block design. Couching braid in the original

Ohio Star

Ohio Star pattern subtly helps the eye to distinguish the base pattern.

Machine couching can be done on the top, prior to quilting, but this can make quilting challenging. It can also be added later as part of the quilting process. By adding it last, couching can help to integrate the machine quilting lines, while adding texture to the quilted surface. I also like the effect of the couched threads or braids sinking more into the surface.

To add a decorative thread, braid, or yarn to the quilted surface (for simplicity, I'll refer to it as a braid), you will need the following supplies:

- a large-eyed hand needle,
- a marking chalk,
- a zigzag sewing machine,
- an open foot for the machine,
- a full bobbin, and a matching cotton, rayon, or metallic thread for the top.

1. First, decide where to place the braid and draw a line with chalk. Make sure the beginning and end of the line are clearly indicated. Do not attempt to pin the braid in place or pre-cut it to length, because both actions may thwart your efforts.

2. Thread the braid through a large-eyed hand needle. At the beginning of the chalk line, poke the needle down from the top at an angle to the back (Fig. 1). The angle of the needle should be almost horizontal, to leave approximately 1" of braid buried in the batting. Remove the needle from the braid and pull the other end of the braid forward so that just a small tail is left on the quilt's back.

3. Set your machine for short, straight stitches. Place your quilt under the machine, centering it where the couching braid appears, and hand lower the needle so it pierces the braid at its center (Fig. 2). Lower your presser foot and make two or three small stitches forward, then back stitch to the beginning. These stitches will hold the braid in place and keep it from slipping.

4. Now set the machine zigzag stitch width just wider than the braid, so it goes into the fabric without catching the braid on either side. Slightly loosen the upper thread tension. Lay the braid down over the chalk line, working just 4" to 5" in front of the foot (Fig. 3), and slowly zigzag the braid into place (Fig. 4). The open foot allows you to see exactly where the needle is stitching, helping you to control the braid placement.

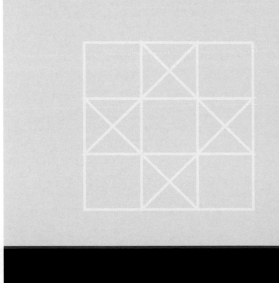

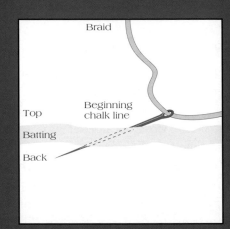

Fig 1. Begin couching by using a needle to pull one end of the braid to the back of the quilt.

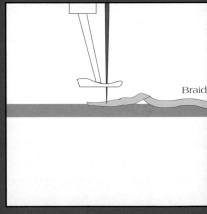

Fig 2. Hand lower the needle to pierce the braid at its center.

Elizabeth Hendricks

5. Stop stitching when about 4" from the end. Carefully measure your braid, allowing at least 3" extra beyond the end of the design. Cut the braid off, and thread it through the hand needle. Then carefully needle it through the top and batting at a horizontal angle toward you and out the quilt's back. Again leave about a 1" tail buried in the batting. From underneath the quilt, pull the braid taut, then resume zigzagging to the design's end.

6. At the end, change the machine setting to a straight stitch and back stitch several small stitches through the center of the braid to secure it.

7. Remove the quilt from the machine. Pull the sewing threads to the back, knot the threads, and with a hand needle, bury the thread ends. Pull the couching braid tail taut from the back, and clip it close to the surface. The braid tail will disappear into the quilt. With a fingernail scratch the hole in the cloth closed.

Once you are comfortable machine couching, you can begin to couch multiple braids beside one another and create grids or wonderful curvilinear shapes. The possibilities are many. Enjoy.

Braid   Chalk line

Fig 3. Lay the braid over the chalk line several inches at a time ahead of stitching.

Fig 4. Zigzag close to the edges.

Elizabeth Hendricks

Ohio Star

STAR LIGHT, STAR BRIGHT

50" x 50", Cotton/polyester blends
Strip piecing over paper

Jane Lloyd

Jane Lloyd Ballymaen, Co. Antrim, Northern Ireland

MY QUILTMAKING

I started quiltmaking in 1977 when I saw a quilt in a magazine and decided to make one. I had been to art college and worked in different mediums, but I found that this was a perfect medium for me. I used to do it all by hand because I had no confidence on the machine. My friends kept telling me that I could make more quilts if I used the machine, so I practiced and eventually got better. I have found a way of being as accurate as when hand sewing, by sewing over papers, and now I have several machines and an industrial one as well.

I belong to the Northern Ireland Patchwork Guild, which meets once a month, and also belong to a small group called Off Cuts which also meets on regular basis. This small group is great because we all help each other, with everything from taking out basting stitches to giving encouragement.

I continue to work on quilts and enjoy the challenge of completing work for special shows and contests. I like working to dates – it motivates me.

MY QUILT

My quilt was inspired by the MAQS contest. I get an idea in my head, think about it for some time, then begin before I've finished the entire design. The design grows along the way. I knew I wanted to incorporate a large star within the nine blocks, but until the very end, I didn't know how. I didn't want it to show up too much. I wanted people to look into the quilt and find the star. I wanted to blend colors through the quilt diagonally. I am extremely fond of strips, which offer a good way of blending colors. They always seem to come into my quilts in some form, straight or curved. I find endless possibilities through strips. My three daughters, ages 16, 14, and 12, help me with design and color. They are very critical and have great ideas to inspire me.

Close-up of STAR LIGHT, STAR BRIGHT

Ohio Star

OHIO STAR
patterns

¼" seam allowance included.

Included in this section are 11 different sizes of full patterns for the traditional Ohio Star block. Select the size most appropriate for your fabrics and project plans, and try your own hand at this popular pattern.

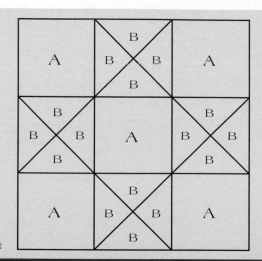

patch
placement

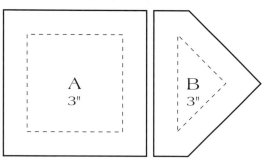

3" BLOCK

4" BLOCK

5" BLOCK

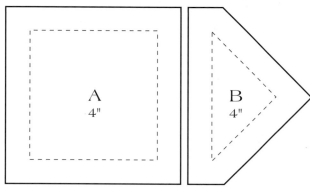

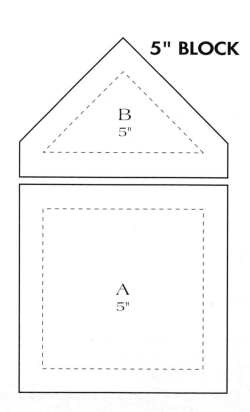

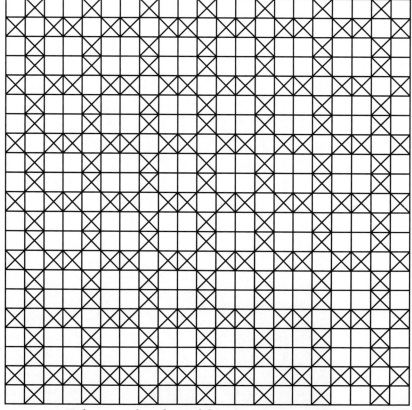

Enlarge grid as desired for planning your quilt.

Ohio Star

OHIO STAR
patterns
¼" seam allowance included.

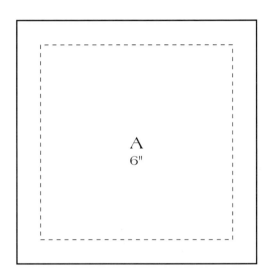

patch placement

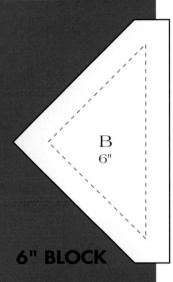

B
6"

A
6"

6" BLOCK

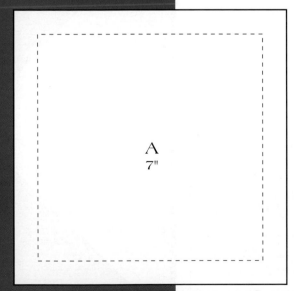

A
7"

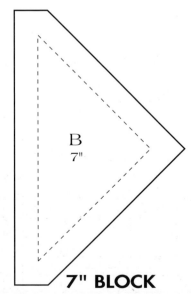

B
7"

7" BLOCK

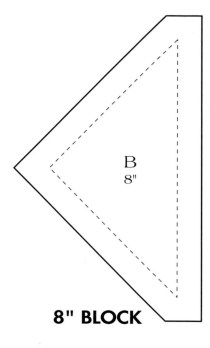

patch placement

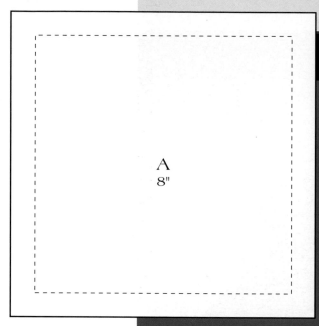

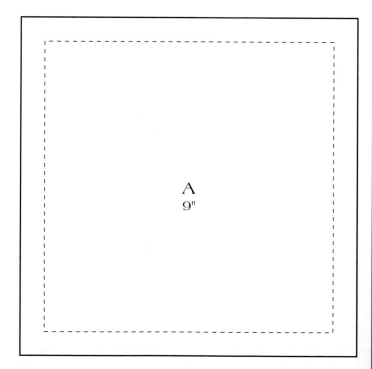

B
8"

A
8"

8" BLOCK

A
9"

B
9"

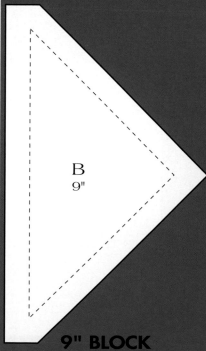

9" BLOCK

EDITOR'S CHOICE New Quilts from an Old Favorite

OHIO STAR
patterns
¼" seam allowance included.

B
10"

10" BLOCK

A
10"

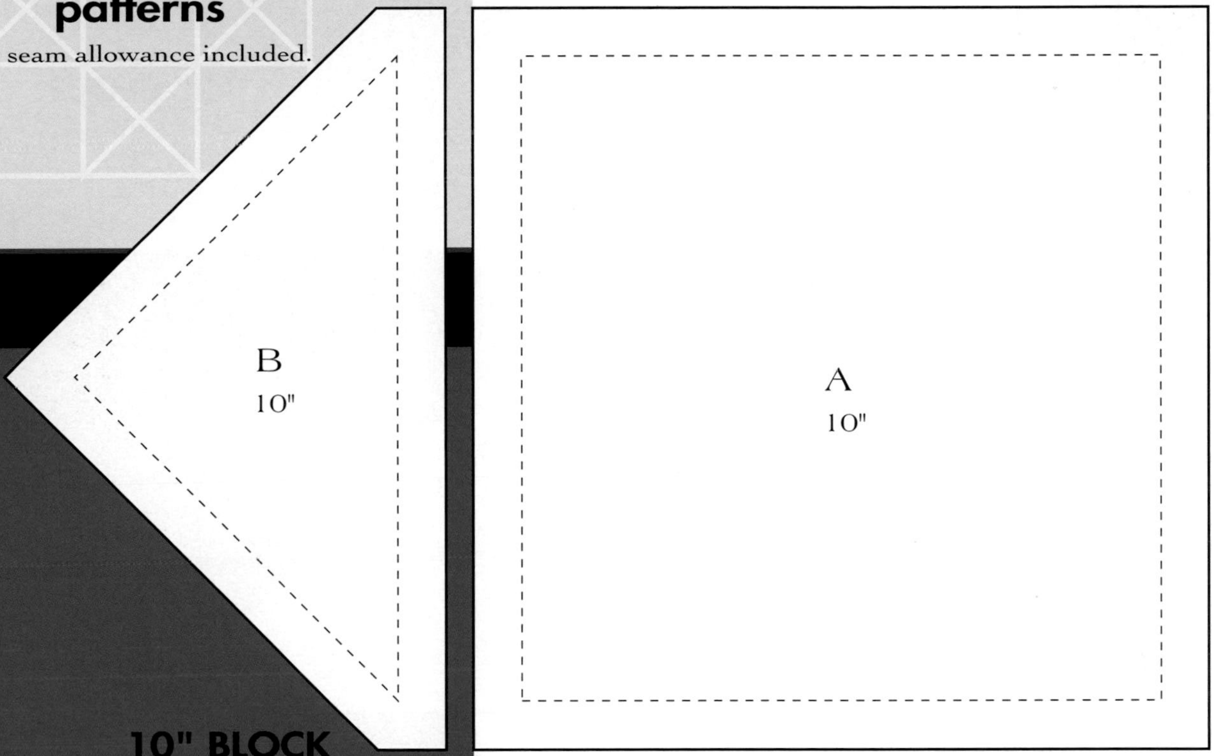

11" BLOCK

A
11"

B
11"

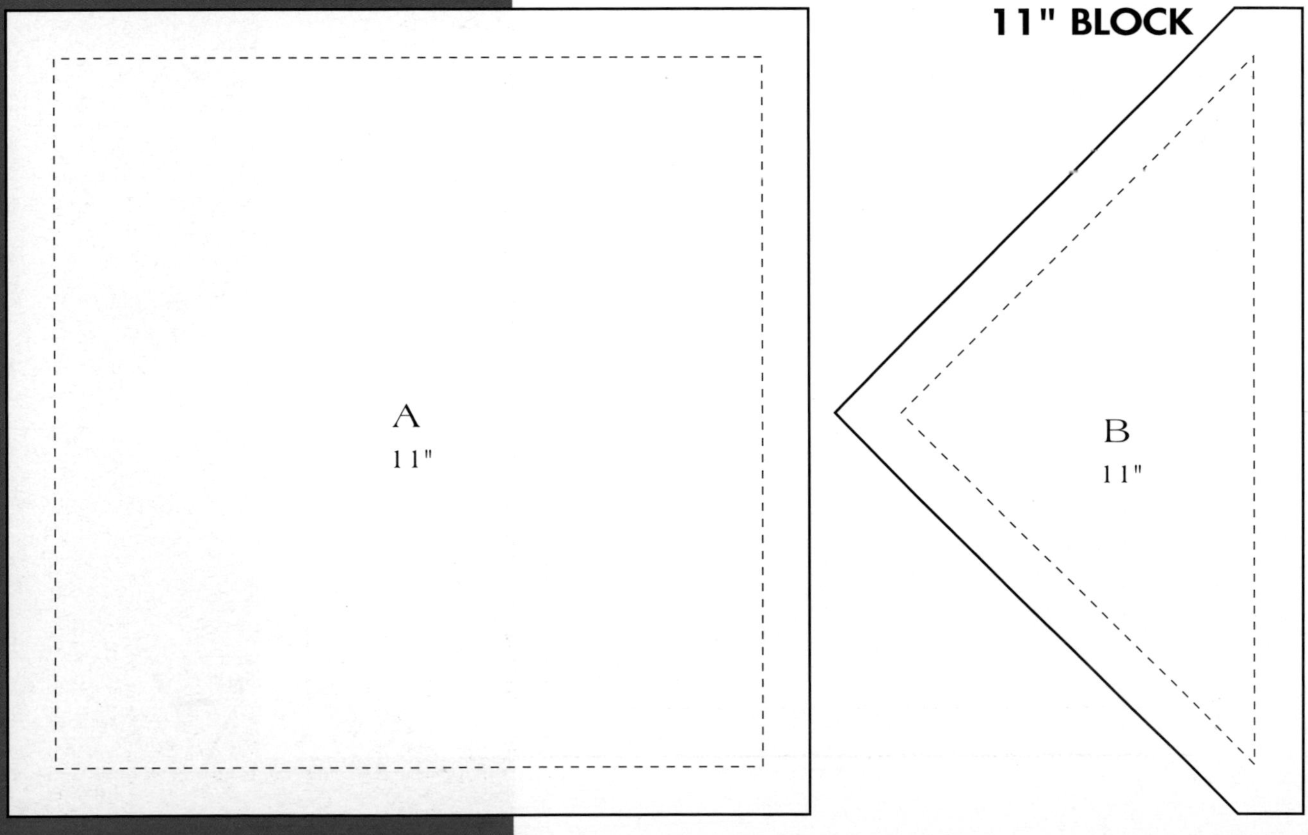

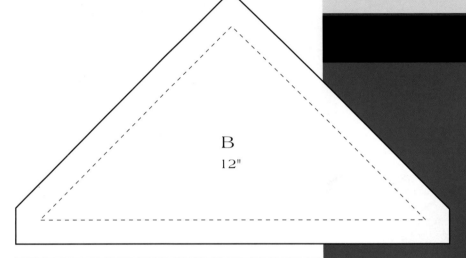

patch placement

OHIO STAR
patterns
¼" seam allowance included.

12" BLOCK

B
12"

A
12"

12" Block

OHIO STAR
patterns
¼" seam allowance included.

14" BLOCK

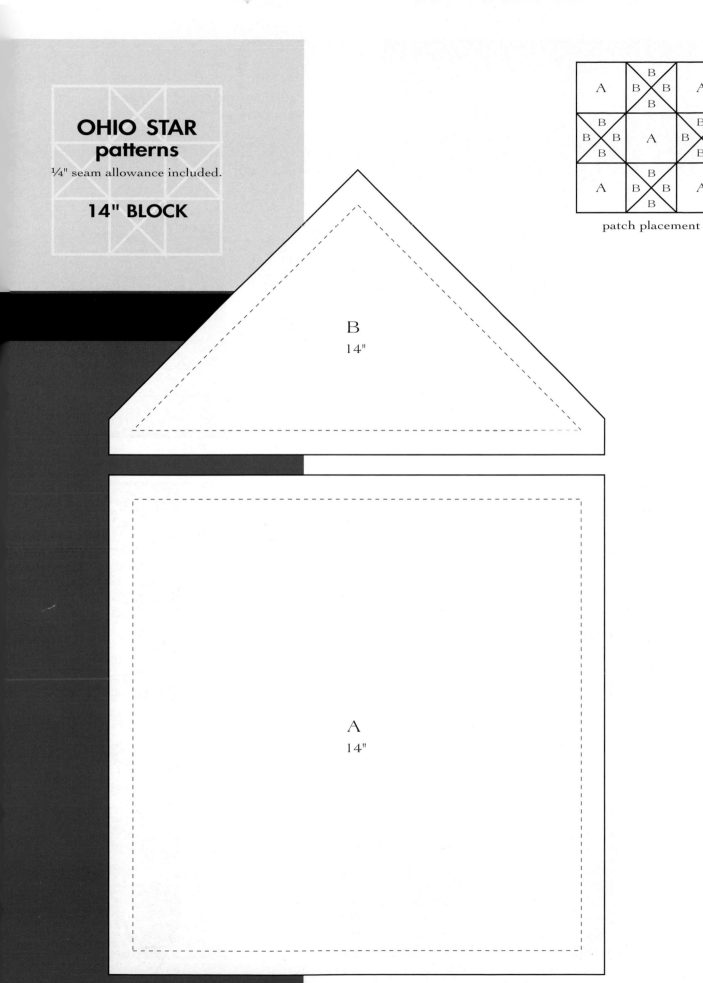

patch placement

B
14"

A
14"

Other AQS Books

This is only a small selection of the books available from the American Quilter's Society. AQS books are known worldwide for timely topics, clear writing, beautiful color photos, and accurate illustrations and patterns. The following books are available from your local bookseller, quilt shop, or public library.

#6075   us$24.95

#5296   us$16.95

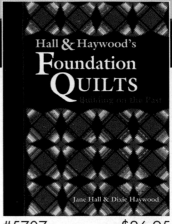

#5707   us$26.95

#6005   us$19.95

#5592   us$24.95

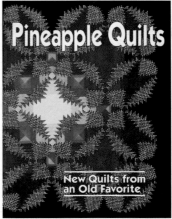

#5098   us$16.95

#6079   us$21.95

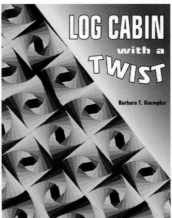

#4545   us$18.95

#5754   us$19.95